The RFU
Handbook of
Safe Rugby

A & C Black • London

First published 1998 by
A & C Black (Publishers) Ltd
35 Bedford Row, London WC1R 4JH

Copyright © 1998 A & C Black (Publishers) Ltd

ISBN 0 7136 4520 2

Acknowledgments
Action photographs courtesy of Colorsport.
Kit photographs on pages 5 and 7 courtesy of
James Gilbert Ltd.
Line drawings by Ron Dixon.

This book has been typeset in Trump Mediaeval 11/12pt
Printed and bound in Great Britain by
Hillman Printers (Frome) Ltd., Somerset.

• CONTENTS •

Foreword by Bill Beaumont **vii**

The contributors viii

Introduction ix

CHAPTER 1
The field of play 1

CHAPTER 2
Equipment and clothing 5

CHAPTER 3
The Laws: making the game safer 9

CHAPTER 4
First Aid and acute care 13
The medical aspects of running a club 15; Pre-match check 17; What to do on the pitch 18; Neck injury 22; Concussion 23; Other injuries 24; The principles of acute injury management 25; Soft tissue injury 26; Fractures and dislocations 27

CHAPTER 5
The management of rugby injuries 29
Principles of later management 30; A review of limb injuries 31; Cervical spine injuries 45; Head injuries 47; Infections 53; Injury prevention 56; Doping and drugs 61

CHAPTER 6

Training principles and the growing rugby player 67

*The growing athlete 68; Growth and strength 69;
Three year rule 71; Overview 71; Muscle groups and joint
movements 72; Muscle tendon balance 73; Co-ordination
patterns 74; Sport-specific techniques 75; Resistance training -
general principles 76; Etiquette 77; Assessment 77; Warm-up 80;
Flexibility 81; Technique 83; Integration 84; Periodisation 85;
Equipment 86; Warm-down 87*

CHAPTER 7

Coaching: good and bad practice 89

*The coach and safety 89; Player preparation 90; The
coach in action 92; The coach and the management team 93;
Coaching awards and qualifications 94*

CHAPTER 8

Technique 97

*Contact with the ground 98; Ball presentation 98; The role of the
first support player 99; The role of other support players 99;
Scrummage 100; Line-out 102; Tackling 102*

CHAPTER 9

The rugby Continuum 107

CHAPTER 10

RFU Personal Accident Insurance Scheme 111

CHAPTER 11

Women's rugby 115

Foreword

Rugby has been a major part of my life, and since 1995 the sport has had to contend with enormous change as it has embraced the professional era.

It has always been a physical sport, one in which body contact is central, so it is not surprising that there are injuries. But rugby is not dangerous. Training programmes have been developed to assist with making the game as safe as possible, and the authorities are constantly considering ways of changing the Laws to make rugby safer.

I am delighted that the RFU has now produced a publication to address the subject of safety within the game. Its *Handbook of Safe Rugby* gives all clubs and players an invaluable insight into the basics of playing the game safely, as well as offering some excellent practical advice on training and techniques.

It is impossible to completely eliminate the risk of injury in a contact sport, but I am sure that all players, particularly at the grass roots of the game, will benefit greatly from reading this handbook and that they will learn how to play, **safely**, the greatest game in the world.

W.B. Beaumont
(National Member of RFU)
Chairman of RFU National Playing Committee

The contributors

CHAPTERS 1 and 2
J.D. Hall
RFU Sports Injuries Administrator

CHAPTER 3
E.J. Blackman
(English Rugby Football Schools Union)
Chairman of RFU Laws Committee

CHAPTERS 4 and 5
N.J. Henderson
RFU Honorary Consultant Surgeon
(mouth-guard section contributed by
W.T. Treadwell, RFU Honorary Dental Surgeon)
Also contributed to *CHAPTER 4:*
A.J. Spreadbury, RFU Panel Referee

CHAPTER 6
D. Gatherer
RFU Honorary Physiotherapist

CHAPTERS 7 and 8
F.A. Biscombe
RFU Divisional Technical Administrator (North)

CHAPTER 9
J.A. Morten
(E. Midlands Rep. of RFU)
Chairman of RFU Playing Development Committee

CHAPTER 10
P. Geraghty
RFU staff member responsible for insurance matters

CHAPTER 11
R. Golby
President of Women's RFU

Introduction

For over 100 years the game of rugby has been played and developed, and has grown enormously in popularity. It is now a professional sport and is played in England in over 3000 schools and 2000 clubs by men and women, girls and boys.

As a contact sport it is not surprising that there are, regrettably, instances of serious injury. Yet considering the numbers playing the game and the enormous spread of ages, capabilities and standards of fitness, the incidence of injury is very low.

The Rugby Football Union (RFU) is the governing body of the sport in England and as such has a duty to care for all those playing rugby. In 1994 the RFU formed the Player Safety Committee in order to focus attention on all rugby safety issues. I have been the Committee's Chairman since its formation. Its terms of reference are as follows.

• To investigate and promote ways of making the game as safe as possible at all age levels.

• To compile statistics of all reported serious injuries which prevent a player from playing or training for 21 or more consecutive days.

• To maintain a register of all former players who are so seriously injured that they are not capable of following a normal existence, and to advise on ways and means of helping them and their dependents.

The Player Safety Committee was spawned out of the old RFU Injuries Working Party which had for some years compiled statistics on rugby injuries. Such statistics are very important because without them it is impossible to recommend changes to the Laws of the Game in order to make the game safer. Even now, although it is mandatory for *all* clubs and schools to make serious injury returns twice a year (in December and April), the response is still disappointing. Remember, it is mandatory for all rugby clubs and schools to report injuries that keep a player out of playing or training for 21 days or more. The Laws of rugby are made by the International Rugby Football Board (IRFB) and all Law changes proposed on safety grounds must be supported by statistical evidence.

Women's rugby is one of the fastest growing sports in this country and is open to all females over the age of 12 years old. Prior to that age rugby is mixed and played to the Laws of the rugby Continuum. The Continuum must be regarded as the coaching pathway by which children are introduced to the game and learn the skills of rugby without being typecast early on as a prop or a scrum-half or a winger. By the gradual build-up of knowledge and skill, children learn to progress safely and with confidence up to the 15-a-side game.

Schools and clubs are equally important in the development of players and through their joint coaching efforts our enormous playing numbers should develop and continue to produce world class athletes who will represent England and make their country the world champions of the future. But only a tiny number make it to the very top.

The vast majority of players will continue as amateurs and play just for fun, although it is not much fun if it is not played safely. Personal safety involves being fit to play. Statistics prove that there is a peak of injuries at the beginning of the season in September because people start playing without training and adequate preparation.

The tackle is proving to be the most likely cause of serious injury, yet the vast majority of such injuries could have been avoided if proper techniques had been employed. Responsible coaching is fundamentally important here, in particular during the development years in clubs and schools.

The RFU Handbook of Safe Rugby is aimed at the inexperienced player, coach, school teacher and administrator, although there may well be some tips that the more experienced could benefit from. It is also aimed at the parent who might be concerned about his son or daughter taking up this contact sport. Although I am not trying to dispel all parental fears of the game, this handbook has been devised to be informative and provide a basic knowledge of equipment and clothing, warm-up and technique, and some insight into coaching.

Rugby is a physically demanding sport which now demands much greater fitness levels as the Laws have evolved in order to increase speed and make it a more open game. Add the element of physical contact and you have a game which potentially could be dangerous if it were not taught, coached and refereed well.

It is the referee's primary responsibility to ensure the safety of players at all times. The players' safety takes precedence over everything else: *if it looks dangerous, the referee will stop it.* The good referee will never compromise safety and will be constantly alert to potential dangers and use the whistle to prevent injury. Foul and dangerous play have no place in the game. The Laws provide all the necessary sanctions, as well as preventative measures, to allow a fair physical contest.

It must be emphasised that rugby is a safe sport. It is impossible to legislate against all injury but the RFU insists that all players are covered by adequate insurance. Therefore all clubs and schools are compelled to cover their teams against accident.

In order to play rugby safely and minimise injury it is important to follow the sound basic rules which are in this handbook. In particular:

• wear regulation clothing and boots, including a fitted mouth-guard
• learn the appropriate techniques for your position and especially how to tackle
• always warm up, and train regularly: it is no good playing rugby if you are unfit
• *never* try to conceal a head injury, and remember concussion results in a three-week mandatory rest *for the player's own safety.*

The most important aspect of the game of rugby is that it is enjoyed, so have fun and play safely.

Captain C.R. Tuffley LVO RN
(RN and RM Rep. of RFU)
Chairman, RFU Player Safety Committee

Note   Throughout this handbook players and officials are referred to individually as 'he'. This should, of course, be taken to mean 'he or she' where appropriate.

CHAPTER 1

The field of play

The pitch

Safe rugby demands a pitch which is level and uniformly covered in grass. The IRFB and the RFU allow clay or sand - provided it is not dangerous - when grass is not available.

The grass should be kept reasonably short and it should be firm enough to withstand the continuous pounding of 30 booted individuals during any one match. It should be able to accommodate between six and eight hours of play each week during the rugby season.

The playing area and its immediate surrounds should be well drained and damage to the surface should be repaired after matches. Regular spiking, rolling and cutting help to preserve the quality of the playing surface.

Pitches situated in public areas such as parks and multi-sport centres should be examined, before play, for dangerous debris and dog mess.

Where no pitch barriers exist, spectators should stand at least 2 metres back from the touch-lines. This allows touch judges to do their jobs and makes the playing situation safer for players and spectators.

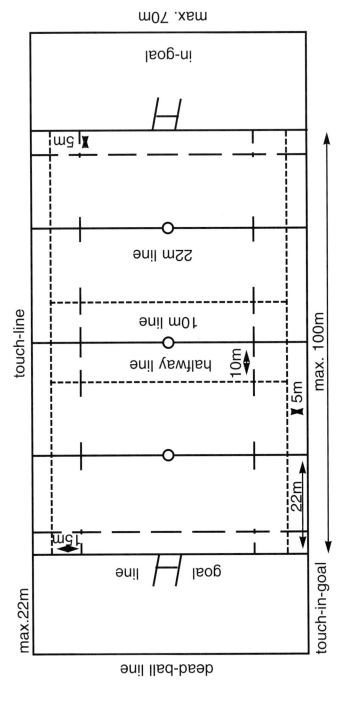

Figure 1 Plan of the playing area

Definitions (IRFB and RFU)

• The **field of play** is the area (as shown in fig.1) between the goal-lines and the touch-lines. These lines are not part of the field of play.

• The **playing area** is the field of play and the in-goals (as shown in fig.1). The touch-lines, touch-in-goal lines and dead-ball lines are not part of the playing area.

• **In-goal** is the area between the goal-line and the dead-ball line, and between the touch-in-goal lines. It includes the goal-line but it does not include the dead-ball line or the touch-in-goal lines.

Posts

Minimum height	3.4 m
Minimum width	5.6 m
Cross bar height	3.0 m

Flags

Minimum height   1.2 m (above ground)

Flags other than those marking corners should be 1 metre back from the touch-line.

Lines

These should be clearly marked in a non-toxic fluid, preferably white.

CHAPTER 2

Equipment and clothing

Equipment

Playing the game

The ball must be made of four panels, though not necessarily of leather.

Length	280–300 mm
Weight	400–440 grams
Circumference at centre	580–620 mm
Circumference end to end	760–790 mm
Pressure	0.66–0.703 kg per sq cm (9.5 lbs per sq inch)

Smaller versions are permitted for younger age groups. Spare balls should be available.

Controlling the game

The game is controlled by a referee and two touch judges. The referee should have: a watch (preferably two); a whistle (preferably two); a notebook and pencil; a coin for the toss. The touch judges should have a flag each to indicate decisions or to give advice to the referee.

First Aid cover

General advice about safe practice in games and training is included in the RFU's Player Safety leaflets numbers 1–8. Numbers 5, 6 and 7 deal with First Aid, equipment and managing very serious injuries. These pamphlets may be obtained from:

The Resource Centre
Rugby Football Union
Nortonthorpe Mills
Scissett
Huddersfield
West Yorkshire
HD8 9LA.

While it is not intended to reproduce the contents of these pamphlets in this handbook, certain essential information regarding safety equipment should be noted by all clubs and schools.

There should be an up-to-date First Aid bag or box adjacent to the playing pitch(es). It must be easily available for use by persons familiar with its content and their application.

There should be a lightweight stretcher in close proximity to the pitches being used.

Telephone communication - either portable or permanent - should be readily accessible to all the pitches being used.

Remember: in all cases of suspected very serious injuries, players should not be moved unless by qualified medics or paramedics.

Clothing

Players may wear a shirt or jersey made of conventional strong and soft material. The shirt or jersey should be marked in club colours which allow for easy recognition.

Certain games demand that numbers should be clearly indicated on the rear of the shirt or jersey.

Advertising logos most conform to the current regulations issued by the IRFB and the RFU.

Players' shorts should be made of a strong, pliable material.

Socks are recommended to protect the players' legs and to produce a comfort barrier between feet and boots.

Boots must also conform to the regulations laid down by the IRFB and the RFU. These regulations can change even in mid-season. Studs or bars should not have sharp edges which could cause injury.

Players must not:
• wear rings or bracelets during games or practice
• wear harness-type shoulder pads
• wear braces or rigid supports which include rigid or reinforced material.

Players may wear the following types of padding and protective clothing, providing it meets the specifications included in the revision of Law 4 issued by the IB from 2 March 1998:

• elasticated bandages
• shin-guards
• ankle supports
• fingerless gloves
• mouth-guards
• shoulder pads
• head-guards.

Replacement players should wear a tracksuit or additional warm clothing while waiting near the touch-line.

CHAPTER 3

The Laws:
making the game safer

At the 1997 World Conference of International Players, Referees, Coaches and Law Makers, the conference facilitator compiled a list of headings comprising the areas of interest of these distinguished representatives. The list was quite lengthy, and situated almost at the bottom was the word safety. Each delegate was then asked to prioritise the various recommendations. Safety was immediately promoted to the top of the list.

That all the delegates reacted in such a way did not mean that they were participants in a violent, uncontrolled activity masquerading as an international sport. In fact the opposite was true: they knew that in a highly competitive sport where bodily contact was frequent, it was essential for a code of Laws to exist so that the players could perform to the best of their ability without fear of deliberate acts of foul play.

A second recommendation of the conference suggested that, provided the Laws were enforced by the referee and obeyed by the players, there would be increased continuity in play and, probably, a reduction in injuries in contact situations.

In many ways the referee is like a teacher in charge of a class- he is in *loco parentis*. No parent willingly puts his or her child in danger, quite the reverse. By using their senses they anticipate possible dangers and take appropriate action. Sometimes the warning signals are easily detected and a slow, subtle approach can avert future problems. On other occasions immediate action needs to be taken without thought to the future. In many ways the advantage lies with the parents as they are generally dealing with one or two children. The teacher frequently has to deal with 30 or so inquiring minds, all of whom want their problems answered immediately. The referee has similar problems except that he's frequently dealing with 30 highly-motivated athletes who may or may not want to perform within the Laws of the game.

In recent years the team coach has achieved a position of authority in relation to how players play and teams perform. It frequently follows that it is the coach who dictates the style of play used by a team and how a player performs to contribute to that style. At the highest levels of the game there are specialist coaches for all facets of the game: scrum, line-out, tackling, kicking, running, fitness, weight training, etc., all supported by expert medical teams. This contrasts with the volunteer parent or former player who has been enlisted to help the youngster in the club to play and enjoy his rugby at mini, midi, junior or youth level. They may seem a world apart but they have a shared responsibility for how they interpret the spirit of the game. They cannot control the single violent act of a player, but they can, through preparation and influence, indicate to those under their charge what is acceptable and what is not.

Long before the coach achieved such a position of influence a school teacher with responsibility for a first XV asked his newly-elected captain what he thought of the prospects of the forthcoming season. After some time the captain suggested a modest prediction of a 50% success rate. He was somewhat surprised to be told that provided his players could read and understand simple English, the master would provide the wherewithal to secure a 75% return. The teacher then produced a pile of RFU booklets entitled 'Why the whistle went' and added while handing them over, 'If your team can answer that question we'll be successful this season'. The players did their bit and the teacher's promise was achieved.

An enterprising player might consider producing a booklet for referees and spectators entitled 'What I'm trying to do on the rugby field'. It might be necessary to have two authors of such a pamphlet since the playing targets of the elegant England centre, Jeremy Guscott, might differ from those of 'Ripper' Smith, the less elegant prop of the Dockers RFC third XV. However, if the referee had a clear understanding of what Jeremy and Ripper were about, he could act and referee accordingly.

The onset of the professional game has seen dramatic changes in the lines of communication among national coaches and national leagues, coaches, referees and law makers in England. There are meetings at which problems of implementation and interpretation are aired and, hopefully, solutions agreed. In an attempt to obtain universal refereeing consistency, the referees of the northern and southern hemispheres are involved in frequent exchanges. No longer will players look at the list of match officials and exchange opinions on 'Ball in straight at scrum and line-out – dream on baby'; 'Release the ball immediately at the tackle – you've got to be joking'; 'Obstruction – anything goes'; 'Slow dawdle back in defence – he never spots it'.

There is no doubt that the present referees at the highest level are doing their utmost to achieve the correct balance between continuity and the battle for possession. In the era of world television coverage of all sports, rugby is no different to any other sport: the young and impressionable will emulate the stars on TV. If our top players and officials get it right in performance and behaviour, then the game will flourish.

There are various areas in our game which give cause for concern. The first deals with protective clothing. The RFU tried to follow the IRFB's Laws to the letter, but saw its players disadvantaged when their opponents were dressed in equipment which clearly contradicted IB Laws. In order to compete on equal terms, our players in the national teams wore similar garments. Having seen their heroes on television, club players immediately cried foul when the referee of their game gave them marching orders if they persisted in wearing protective clothing. The position has now been clarified and protective clothing, clearly defined, is now allowed. These garments are expensive, with head-guards and padded vests being particularly costly. It would be a tragedy if young people wanting to play rugby were to be disadvantaged if they could not afford all the playing kit which was deemed to be necessary.

There is no doubt the quality of possession obtained in the line-out has improved since supporting the jumper has been permitted. However, the height achieved by the jumper, plus the possible interference of those giving support to the ball winner, does give cause for concern. As yet the IB has not given a lead as to when this activity is best introduced to youngsters, so the RFU has introduced a domestic Law which forbids support being given in all matches at Under-15 and below. This domestic Law has been adopted by Ireland and is being considered by the other Home Unions, with safety being a prime concern.

The third area concerns the difficulty encountered by defenders when faced by a driving maul. It has been a maxim of our game that the ball carrier can be tackled. However, this is impossible if the ball carrier is at the rear of the maul and his colleagues who are in contact with their opponents are driving towards their line.

This problem has exercised the minds of law makers, players, coaches and referees, but as yet we have been unable to find a safe solution. Any suggestions would be greatly received at Twickenham.

For the last two years the RFU has received the co-operation of Cambridge University Rugby Club in trialling a wide and varied series of experimental Laws in the inter-college matches. This CURFC Laws Laboratory has enabled the Laws Committee to enlist the views of players, coaches, referees and match observers in the trialled Law experiments with particular reference to safety, open play and constructive variations of the present Laws. It must be stressed that the safety of the players has been at the forefront of all these experiments, with a careful trial and screening process before their introduction.

This is indicative of the positive approach being taken by all involved in the game. The desire to play in a game which gives full reign to all players to participate in a free-flowing activity, yet still retains the physical confrontation for possession and the mastery of skills to obtain that possession, in a safe and controlled environment, only needs the shared vision of players, coaches, referees and law makers. The wonderfully vibrant match between England and the All Blacks in December 1997 showed what a marvellous game rugby can be when played in the manner requested by the international conference referred to at the beginning of this chapter.

CHAPTER 4

First Aid and acute care

Rugby is a tough, physical game. It is likely that players may sustain knocks, bruises, strains and abrasions. Indeed, players risk occasional serious injury.

With increasing awareness and application of fitness and training techniques, players are becoming fitter, faster, stronger and more competitive. A more vigorous approach is evident which is not confined to the upper levels but filters down through the game as a whole, particularly to the schools. The Laws and approach to the game demand more action and less rest. The front five have to be mobile and the back line have to be increasingly involved in close contact. The new professional age is forcing increased demands on players at the top end of the game, with less time for recuperation and recovery between an intensive programme of matches or at the end of the season.

It becomes increasingly likely that injuries will not only occur as a result of acute episodes on the pitch or in training but also as a result of over-use and the failure to let minor knocks recover before subjecting them to further trauma. There are many factors which may lead to injury.

Firstly, there are external, or extrinsic, factors which affect the player. The most obvious of these would be a blow that may lead to a cut or a broken bone; or an awkward fall or twist that may lead to a torn ligament. The player may be subjected to poor training methods with insufficient warm-up, making him more susceptible to trauma. A poor surface, such as hard road for running, particularly in old or poorly-designed shoes, will lead to repetitive strain on the feet or shins. Inadequate clothing or warm-up during cold weather will lead to stiffness and loss of flexibility.

Secondly, there are internal, or intrinsic, factors which are more concerned with the make-up of the player. For example, adolescents may be more prone to certain patterns of over-use injury, particularly around the knee: training programmes may have to be adjusted to take account of this. Older players lose the power of recovery and injuries more readily become chronic. Muscle strain often results from muscle imbalance following previous injury which is not yet recovered or is simply a consequence of being unfit. Joints which are too lax or too stiff are at risk and muscle stabilisation programmes or stretching techniques must be applied. Poor alignment, particularly of the feet, can put extra strain on the lower limb during prolonged running.

Many of these factors combine to result in over-use injuries. Players must learn to recognise the signs and coaches must come to terms with the consequences if ignored. The causes are greater load or repetitive activity, often aggravated by poor technique and poor posture.

At the extreme, bone may suffer an overt stress, or fatigue fracture. Joints and ligaments become stiff and strained and tendons may become chronically inflamed. It is important to recognise what is happening to permit appropriate treatment, rather than trying to push through the problem. Akin to over-use injury is the over-training syndrome resulting from failure to include proper rest during training programmes and the repetitive stress of training in competition. This results in fatigue depression and under-performance. These factors themselves will precipitate further injuries.

Thus there are many factors concerned with the assessment and management of injuries which extend beyond the simple treatment of a bruise or cut.

The general management of injuries follows certain basic principles through the acute phase, the diagnosis and definition of injury, and the later rehabilitation. The acute management in the context of the serious injury requires some knowledge of how to save life and some understanding of serious spinal and head trauma. Much can go wrong with the early management of lesser injuries. It is important that the approach is right from the beginning to set the scene for a prompt and complete recovery. Recovery does not end with simple healing of the injury but must extend through general rehabilitation, restoration of fitness and training. Complete recovery from an injury implies that the player is fully match fit and the responsibility of the medical professionals extends through to this point. The player must get fit to play: he should not play to get fit.

First Aid
(1) Maintain life.
(2) Prevent secondary or more extensive injury.
(3) Promote recovery.

The medical aspects of running a club

Rugby clubs vary enormously in their size, location and resources. Top clubs in the new professional era are starting to employ full-time physiotherapists and may have a team of doctors and others to look after their players. At the other end of the spectrum, informal groups of amateurs may meet occasionally on a pitch without facilities. Yet the game is essentially the same. It is a physical contest played to the same rules and the risk of injury may not vary greatly.

There is an increasing need to provide some form of medical back-up or at least to establish a safety net if injury is sustained. Players, and in particular parents, are more appreciative of risk and clubs are becoming increasingly aware of legal liability. However, it is the very variation in clubs and schools which makes it difficult to stipulate what the facilities should be. Nevertheless, even in the presence of skilled medical care, communications and the ability to summon help are the key to safe practice.

At every club or playing venue there must be:
• a telephone
• ambulance access.

A member of every team should know where the nearest telephone is. Mobile phones must be tested to ensure that the local signal is sufficiently strong. Ideally adjacent to a fixed phone, there should be a register with the number of the local hospital and each club should keep a list of players' home telephone numbers to inform relatives if there has been any accident. Few clubs will be able to provide sophisticated medical support: the aim is to keep the player safe until he can be transferred to hospital.

Medical facilities

Ideally, within a club house there should be a designated quiet room where the players can rest or be assessed away from the well-meaning and inquisitive. The room should contain clean running water, good lighting, good heating and be close to the telephone. If

15

there is no club house there should be a sheltered area close to the pitch where a player who can be moved can rest and wait for further assistance.

The medical area should contain the equipment outlined on page 18. If a doctor is in regular attendance there will be the facility for cleaning and suturing small wounds, and applying dressings, bandages and splints. There must be good access to the medical area for ambulance stretchers.

Increasing use is being made of stand-by ambulances at rugby grounds. During a busy afternoon there may be many teams playing and many spectators. It is prudent to have an ambulance standing by and those organising tournaments, such as minis festivals, should seriously consider this. Indeed, if there is likely to be an attendance of more than 4,000 it is a legal requirement. If there is likely to be an attendance of more than 2,000 there is an obligation to have a doctor available. Ambulances can be arranged through the local ambulance stations, the St. Johns Ambulance Service or the Red Cross.

Personnel

Clubs may avail themselves of a variety of medical help. Most may be practitioners turning out as volunteers for the love of the game.

First Aider

This is the most likely individual to have around. Members of the club should be encouraged to complete a course in basic First Aid or at least in basic life support. Information on these can be obtained through the local ambulance service, St. Johns Ambulance Service or the Red Cross. First Aiders are able to advise and supervise until more skilled help or an ambulance arrives. Coaches in particular should be encouraged to complete a course in these skills.

Physiotherapist

Clubs are increasingly linking with local physiotherapists who are skilled in the management of acute soft tissue injury and also have an appreciation of the management of more serious injuries and of basic life support. Interested physiotherapists may attend matches or even training sessions. If this is not possible, many clubs have negotiated access to local private physiotherapists or to sports injuries clinics, who may see players urgently.

Sports therapist

While they do not have the depth or breadth of training of physio-therapists, sports therapists have training in the treatment of sporting injuries and the background to them.

Doctor

The role of the club doctor varies enormously. Most assume the responsibilities from being a member of the club or simply taking an interest in the game. The degree of specific training or skill in injury management may vary but the doctor's role is valuable in assessing and co-ordinating care for the injured player. There are now a number of sports injury diplomas by which doctors may obtain further qualifications in this field, and in larger clubs such individuals lead a team approach to the integrated care of players.

Other professionals

Many larger clubs also have access to masseurs, who may offer considerable help during the recovery phase. Osteopaths and chiro-practors may help with acute injury, particularly to the lumbar spine. Podiatrists may assist with provision of good footwear sup-port and improving the gait pattern. Specific fitness advisors or coaches are available, although this role is often linked with that of physiotherapist or sports therapist.

Pre-match check

The doctor or physiotherapist (or, if not available, whoever else has been delegated to look after medical matters in the team) should check the situation and facilities before a match or training session takes place.

- Is there a telephone?
- Is there access for an ambulance?

Ensure that all the First Aid equipment is in place in the club house, changing room or medical area. Check that the medical bag, which should be robust and waterproof, is well stocked. Frequently the pitch may be some distance away from any medical facility, so the medical bag should be available near the touch-line.

Medical room	Medical bag
Stretcher†	Ice in bags and clean sponge
Cervical collar (range of sizes)†	Gauze swabs
Bandages	PR spray
Felt	Bandages
Slings	Adhesive tape
Ice and bags	Antiseptic cream
Tape underwrap	Vaseline
Adhesive tape	Scissors
Water	Airway†
Towels	Pocket mask (Laerdal type)†
Blankets	Disposable gloves
Embrocation	Bag for soiled dressings
Crutches	

† Only to be used with prior training

Many other items may be included, according to the preference of the medical attendant, the local circumstances, and the sophistication of the set-up. Nevertheless, a check should always be made. Players may have used all the tape or lost the scissors before the match.

A member of the team should organise drinks for half-time. There may be considerable fluid and salt loss during a training session or match, particularly during hot weather. This fluid loss will affect performance and judgement, and may even predispose to injury. To replace this with water alone can be dangerous. If more than a small drink at half-time is anticipated, then a proprietary isotonic drink, containing salt and other electrolytes, must be used. In hot climates it is permitted to come to the side of the pitch to have a drink during the course of the match.

What to do on the pitch

If a player is injured and collapses to the ground, the game may stop so that those helping may do so in safety. Players and others will wish to help and one person must take charge. This will be the doctor or physiotherapist if present, but at other levels there should be someone with basic First Aid training available, ideally the coach.

If the player is conscious

Ask simple questions. If there is a response, the questions may become more detailed, requesting information about the location of any pain and difficulties in movement. In particular, direct enquiries should be made about neck injury.

"Do you have any pain in your neck or between the shoulder-blades?"

"Do you feel numbness or pins-and-needles in the arms, legs, or anywhere else?"

A picture of the severity of the injury is built up and a decision has to be made whether it is safe for the player to get himself off the pitch or whether a stretcher is needed to help him. Clearly, if in doubt it is better to take an injury too seriously and leave him where he is until the skilled help is sent for and arrives.

If the player is unconscious

The first responsibility is to maintain life by following the well-established protocol:

A - Airway
B - Breathing
C - Circulation.

Firstly, to secure the airway, remove the mouth-guard and any dirt from the mouth. If the player is already on his side in the recovery position, it is probable that the wind-pipe will be clear. However, if there is still airway obstruction, the most likely cause is that the tongue is blocking the entrance to the wind-pipe in the back of the throat. This is much more likely if the unconscious player is lying on his back when the tongue falls backwards. Lift the jaw forwards, which lifts the tongue away from the wind-pipe. If the player is still choking, tilt the head back slightly, but not more than 10°, in case there is a spinal injury. If the player vomits, put him into the recovery position.

Next, look to see if the chest is moving or whether you can hear or feel any breathing. If you can, check the circulation. Continue to check both of these regularly until help arrives.

If there is no breathing, start 'rescue breathing' for the player. The First Aid bag should contain an airway. The Laerdal mask is preferable to the Brook airway. Turn the player on to his back and apply the mask, which covers the nose, or insert the airway, taking care to keep the tongue up and forwards.

Figure 2 Securing the airway

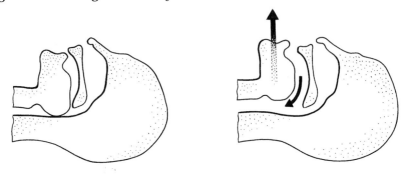

Figure 3 The Brook airway (left) and Laerdal mask (right)

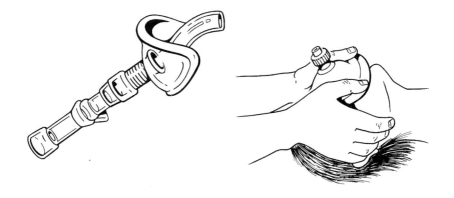

Figure 4 'Rescue breathing' using the Laerdal mask

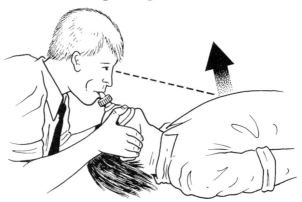

In this case, the nose must be gently pinched to close it. Lift the chin to clear the back of the throat. Give two effective breaths. Little resistance should be encountered to the breath, which will take 1.5–2 seconds. Watch the chest rise and wait for it to fall completely between breaths, which will take 2–4 seconds.

Following these two rescue breaths, check for signs of circulation, feeling for the carotid pulse in the neck which lies adjacent to the wind-pipe. If a pulse is present, continue with rescue breathing and check the pulse every minute.

If there is no sign of circulation, start external cardiac compressions. Place the heel of one hand over the lower half of the sternum (breast-bone), not the ribs or upper abdomen. Place the other hand on top of the first, interlocking the fingers. Having positioned yourself vertically above the victim's chest, hold the elbows straight and press on to the sternum enough to depress it 4–5cm. Pressure should be firm and controlled, and applied at a rate of 100 times per minute. For children external cardiac compressions will need less pressure and should be more frequent.

It is essential to combine ventilation with external cardiac compression in order that the circulating blood is carrying oxygen. It is possible to do both yourself by swiftly changing positions, but it is more efficient to have help. After 15 chest compressions give two effective breaths and then restart the compressions, repeating this cycle until skilled assistance arrives.

If an ambulance has already been sent for and the player's condition deteriorates, immediately phone the ambulance a second time to alert them to the situation. There may be a way they can arrange help more quickly than originally anticipated.

Remember, if you do not attempt cardio-pulmonary resuscitation the player has much less chance of survival.

This is no more that an outline guide to basic life-saving techniques. **To do this properly requires training.**

Every club should have trained members who can be present at matches. You may think you can do it, but an emergency situation is different and more difficult. Contact your local ambulance station, the St. Johns Ambulance Service or the Red Cross for information on basic life support courses.

21

Neck injury

Even apparently minor neck injuries may be serious. If there is any doubt about the neck, it should be treated as a serious injury. If it seems to be no more than a blow or a strain, the player should come off and seek immediate medical attention.

Serious neck injury
• Severe pain in the neck.
• Pain radiating into the arms.
• Numbness in the arms, trunk or legs.
• Weakness in the arms or legs.

If a serious neck injury is suspected, the player should be moved as little as possible, preferably only once and then by trained personnel. Never twist the head and never sit or stand the player up. It must be presumed that any unconscious player has injured his neck. So long as the unconscious player is breathing, he need not be moved, although it is wise to clear the mouth-guard and any dirt in the mouth. However, if the airway is still obstructed after this, it may be necessary to move him, in which case apply a collar first. Move the player very carefully with help, which should be under your command. Keep the head, neck and chest alignment consistent as the player is turned.

There is clearly a concern that a neck injury may be exacerbated. However, though paralysis is a tragedy, failure to carry out adequate ventilation in cases of respiratory arrest will result in death.

**If a player is not breathing,
think spinal, but secure the airway.**

Figure 5 A neck collar (e.g. Necloc, Stiffneck)

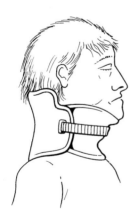

Concussion

Concussion occurs when the brain is injured following a blow to the head or the face. It is important to realise that a player may be concussed without having been unconscious. It may be difficult at times to decide whether a player has been concussed or not, but it is clear that if there is any doubt about the diagnosis, it is safer to presume that he has been. There are many signs and symptoms of concussion, the presence of any of which may be sufficient to make the diagnosis.

Concussion
- Loss of consciousness.
- Confusion and disorientation.
- Double or blurred vision.
- Giddiness or unsteadiness.
- Vomiting.

If the player has lost consciousness it is obvious that he has been concussed. However, if the loss of consciousness is only momentary, the player may have recovered by the time anyone arrives on the scene. Ask the player questions that he ought to be able to answer, such as: What team are you playing?; What is the score?; What half of the game is it? Being unaware of what happened, even for a few moments, at the time of the injury is the most consistent sign that a player has been concussed.

If a player displays any of these characteristics, he should stop training or playing immediately and be taken off the field for medical attention.

If a trained medical attendant is certain that a concussed player has not actually been knocked out and he makes a full recovery in a few moments, he still must not return to play. He may be observed and allowed to go home with head injury instructions and someone to look after him. He should not be allowed to drive or to leave the area unattended.

Head injury instructions
The patient
- Rest quietly at home.
- Avoid strenuous activity.
- Do not drink alcohol.
- Avoid heavy meals.
- Return immediately to the A & E Department if you vomit or if you develop a headache which is not relieved by rest or simple pain-killers.

The person looking after the patient
• If the victim develops increasing drowsiness, has a fit, or develops any unusual symptoms, such as blurring of vision, take them back to the A & E Department immediately.

If the player has been knocked out, if there is any concern whatsoever, or if there is no trained medical personnel, the player should be taken to hospital for a check-up. No player should be left alone, given alcohol, or allowed to drive a vehicle until after medical assessment of their head injury or concussion.

It is important to remember that potentially serious complications can develop many hours after an apparently minor head injury. It is for this reason that anyone suffering concussion should have somebody with them.

The signs and symptoms of complications developing due to deteriorating head injury are:

• persistent headache
• drowsiness leading to unconsciousness
• irritability
• confusion and a loss of concentration
• vomiting
• convulsions.

Players who have suffered concussion or loss of consciousness may not train or play for *at least* three weeks. They may only do so then after they have undergone a neurological examination by a doctor (Regulation 13.6). It is important to realise that the effects of concussion may be prolonged, and to return to training, and particularly contact, too soon can have serious consequences. There is clear medical evidence that a player should be completely symptom-free before returning to training (without contact) and that he should be able to undertake full training for a week without the occurrence of any symptoms before contact or playing.

Other injuries

Players should be dissuaded from continuing to play or train after an injury. A premature return may often aggravate the injury and prolong eventual recovery.

A player should be removed from the pitch if there is any concern about serious injury, particularly to the head and neck areas. It is also mandatory to remove a player to attend to an open, bleeding wound. Remember, the attendant must wear disposable gloves to avoid contaminating the wound and to protect himself from any transmissible infection (*see* page 53). Any blood-soiled clothes must be exchanged before returning to the pitch (Law 4. 2).

While a player who leaves the field because of injury may not return and must be substituted for the rest of the match, a player who leaves to attend to a bleeding wound may be temporarily substituted and may return himself to play (Law 3.6).

The principles of acute injury management

The correct management of an injury must start immediately. The outcome and the speed of recovery are directly related to the quality of the immediate and early care. The player must not continue playing with an injury. This will only increase bruising, tissue damage, later scarring, and prolong recovery.

Assessment	• History
	• Examination
Treatment	• Acute phase
	• Rehabilitation

The first thread that runs through the management of an injury is one of assessment, taking account of the history of the injury together with any contributing factors. Coupled with examination of the injury, this may lead to a diagnosis of exactly what is wrong. The more specific the diagnosis, the more targeted the treatment can be. The second thread is the treatment, both in the acute phase and subsequent treatment, coupled with rehabilitation.

A detailed, blow-by-blow history of how an injury occurred may help us better understand the injury. Information may be gathered at the site of the accident even by those who are not medically qualified, which can help in subsequent medical assessment. To find out exactly what happened, ask the player while his memory is fresh and also ask any witnesses. This is particularly important if the player is concussed.

Make a note if there is an opportunity. For example, the way someone twists and what is felt while injuring a knee can tell a good deal about the disruption inside the joint. A ruptured Achilles tendon is almost always accompanied by the story that the ankle was hit from behind. It is very rare that the ankle has been struck, but this is typically what it feels like, and gives a strong indication that the tendon is actually broken.

The first stage of detailed examination is observation. For example, the rate that a knee swells may indicate whether there is blood inside (it swells almost immediately) or whether there is simply fluid accumulation in response to irritation (it swells overnight). This is important information for diagnosis. The presence of blood clearly indicates a serious injury such as a rupture of the anterior cruciate ligament. Swelling overnight, from fluid, may still be serious but it is less urgent to seek medical attention.

Having looked at the shape, posture, bruising, abrasions and cuts around the injured part, the player may try some gentle active movements which he initiates himself. With his co-operation, passive movements initiated by the examiner may also be tried to test whether these are painful. The injured area can be carefully felt ('palpated') for tender areas. It is important to note whether there is good circulation to the injury and whether there is normal nerve function, i.e. movement and feeling.

For example,with a broken elbow it is important to know whether there is a radial pulse at the wrist and whether there is normal feeling throughout the hand.

Clearly, the degree to which a medical attendant can or should examine an injury will depend on training and experience. Further management will be prescribed on the basis of an accurate diagnosis by a doctor or physiotherapist. X-rays, detailed scans and further investigations may be required.

Soft tissue injury

Injuries to the soft tissues - that is, the skin, subcutaneous fat layers, muscles, tendons, ligaments and joint capsules - swell rapidly. There is local bruising and bleeding into the tissue and a secondary accumulation of fluid. This cannot be rubbed, run off, stretched or manipulated away. The key to immediate management is **RICE** (**R**est, **I**ce, **C**ompression, **E**levation).

- **Rest.** This is important to prevent further soft tissue damage and re-injury.

- **Ice.** This cools the injured part and decreases bruising. Apply crushed ice in a bag, or a proprietary ice gel, for 20 minutes. To prevent an ice burn, make sure there is a layer of towel between the ice and the skin. Another efficient method of application is to use an inflatable cuff filled with iced water.

• **Compression.** This will reduce bleeding and bruising when applied locally to the injury. Use cotton wool or similar padding over the injury and around the joints to spread and even out the pressure, and to protect pressure points. Apply crêpe bandage over this. The pressure must be firm but not so tight as to restrict the overall circulation in the limb. *Never* use a tourniquet.

• **Elevation.** Elevation will reduce the perfusion pressure of blood and so reduce bleeding. It will also ensure that the tissue fluid and swelling can run away out of the injured part back into the circulation. For example, when sitting normally with a swollen foot on the floor, the foot will act as a sump for all the bruising. Elevate the foot above the bottom and the swelling can run off.

Never soak an injury in a very hot bath. The heat will cause vessels to dilate and increase bleeding and bruising. The RICE regime should continue while seeking advice and treatment from a physiotherapist, who will re-introduce movement (to avoid stiffness) and other techniques of soft tissue management.

Fractures and dislocations

It may be difficult to distinguish between a soft tissue injury and a broken bone (a fracture). A severe fracture or a dislocation is usually more obvious because of deformity which is clear to see. If there is any doubt about the severity of the injury, the player must be medically assessed or referred to hospital for X-ray.

The management of a broken bone depends on the severity of the injury. If there is a minor break, for example of the wrist, and the player is able to walk after a few moments, he can be removed from the pitch and taken from there to hospital. If he is unable to walk it may be possible to move the player carefully on to a stretcher and take him to shelter while arranging transport. However if there is a major break with obvious marked deformity, for example a thigh bone, it will be safer to leave the player where he is while summoning skilled help. Remember to keep him warm.

A dislocation usually results in deformity. In rugby the commonest are dislocations of finger-joints. Some players suffer recurrent dislocations of finger-joints and will pull them back into line themselves. Shoulder dislocation is also common and while the deformity may not be that obvious, it is clear that a major injury has been sustained because of marked pain and immobility. The arm should be supported with a sling until the player reaches hospital.

Attempts to reduce dislocations should not be made on the pitch. It is impossible to know whether there is an associated fracture complicating the situation. In the case of finger dislocations, if the joint has been put back the player must still attend hospital for X-ray and medical review.

Occasionally, in association with a dislocation and particularly in association with a broken bone, there may be a wound. Very rarely the bone may be showing through the wound. Do not attempt to replace the bone into the wound. Remove any obvious grass or dirt from the surface and apply a clean dressing with antiseptic solution.

If the player may need to go to hospital due to his injury, do not give him drinks or food. He may need a general anaesthetic which cannot normally be administered within 4–6 hours of oral intake.

Pain-killers

If drink is allowed, pain-killing tablets may be given. Paracetamol is effective as a simple pain-killer (analgesic). Non-steroidal anti-inflammatory analgesics (NSAID) such as Ibuprofen reduce pain by reducing inflammation, and may be helpful during recovery. Beware of using NSAID if there is a history of asthma, which can be made worse, or if there is a history of ulcers or stomach irritation, which can be aggravated as well.

Pain-killers must never be taken to mask pain in order to permit training or playing. This will only make the underlying injury worse.

CHAPTER 5

The management of rugby injuries, and other medical concerns

The principles of First Aid to save life, and an introduction to the acute management of injuries, are outlined in the previous chapter. However, the care of the player and his injury does not stop when he is removed from the pitch. Those who become involved, not only doctors but also physiotherapists and coaches, must work together as a team to see the player through the injury and subsequent rehabilitation. He will need guidance on regaining fitness, while at the same time undergoing specific treatment and focused rehabilitation for his recovering injury. He will need advice about when it is safe to return to play and any precautions that he should take.

The physiotherapist is often central in this team approach, being able to translate strict medical instructions and needs into a practical approach that the coach can work with to keep the player moving towards regaining fitness.

This chapter gives an introduction to some of the more common injuries and medical conditions associated with rugby, but it is beyond the scope of this book to provide a detailed account of all injuries. The nature and management of these common injuries therefore provide examples to highlight general principles. Moreover, there is no sense in talking about injury without reference to injury prevention and it is inevitable that when talking of sport and medicine there should be some mention of drugs and their abuse, provided here at the end of the chapter.

Principles of later management

Whatever the specific requirements of the injury, the player needs supervision during recovery. He will be anxious about the nature of the injury and the implications for recovery and his return to playing. He needs information and explanation at each stage of recovery. An injury should not be regarded simply as time lost, but may be taken as an opportunity to deal with other chronic or over-use injuries which could benefit from rest or treatment. Indeed, while the injured part is being rehabilitated it is essential to main-tain fitness of the rest of the body, not only in strength but also aero-bically.

The physiotherapist uses many techniques during the evolving phases of treatment, rehabilitation and fitness work. Initially, dif-ferent forms of massage are effective for soft tissue injury, reducing swelling, relieving muscle spasm and tightness and improving tone. Deep friction massage may restore mobility and release deep scarring. In this early stage applied treatments such as ultrasound, short wave diathermy and interferential may help to relieve the pain and reduce inflammation. Ice is always useful.

While rest is important in the initial phase following injury, pro-longed rest and immobility lead to wasting and shortening of mus-cles, and joint stiffness. Immobilised muscle will weaken very quickly and take a long time to build up strength. Gentle move-ments can usually begin at an early stage following soft tissue injury, and as soon as fracture healing will allow, movement must begin. Active exercises help to restore muscle, and at times passive movement and gentle mobilisation is necessary to regain a range of movement. Manipulation may also be needed.

As rehabilitation progresses, a programme of strengthening exer-cises will be given to follow the warm-up and stretches. Co-ordi-nation exercises are brought in at a later phase to restore the full functional capacity of the injured limb. A classic example of this is the use of a wobble board underneath the ankle to restore control over lateral movements. During this treatment additional taping or strapping of a joint or injured area will give extra support. The final phase of rehabilitation is full fitness work with rugby-specific training.

A review of limb injuries

There are many tissues that make up the musculo-skeletal system, each of which has its own characteristics and pattern of injury and response.

Bone is not inert but is a living tissue which replaces itself slowly. A broken bone is otherwise known as a fracture. Growing children's bones are not as brittle as adult bones and may bend rather than snap. This is known as a greenstick fracture. Children's bones also heal more quickly than adults'.

Articular cartilage is the smooth-gliding surface which is bonded on to the end of a bone within a joint. Two opposing joint surfaces are surrounded by a capsule and the joint is lubricated by a surface coating of fluid; it is not normal for joint fluid to be detectable by clinical examination.

Within the knee there are tough gristle-like fibrocartilage structures which are often referred to as 'cartilage'. The true name for each of these structures is a 'meniscus' and they should not be confused with the articular cartilage.

Ligaments are composed of collagen fibres arranged like a cable, joining bone to bone across a joint to provide stability. Ruptured ligaments may heal on their own or can be repaired, but are never as tight as they were prior to injury. In some cases, as with the knee, the ligament has to be re-constructed with ligament grafts.

Tendons are similar in structure to ligaments, but their function is to connect muscles to bones. A muscle will usually rupture before a tendon; the tendon itself and its coverings may become inflamed or damaged ('tendonitis'). The junction between the flexible tendon and its insertion into rigid bone is also susceptible to recurrent trauma, often as a result of over-use.

Muscle is composed of tiny fibres which are capable of contraction. Different training methods will enhance different types of muscle activity and potential. For peak performance there is a need to balance strength and speed. Muscle is prone to strain or internal tears, particularly at the junction between muscles and tendon. Imbalance between opposing groups of muscles (e.g. quadriceps and hamstrings) and inadequate warm-up and stretching, may lead to injury, which is also more likely to occur when the muscle is unfit or over-fatigued. Direct trauma to muscle will result in bruising and possibly some scarring which predisposes to muscle tears unless care is taken.

A **bursa** is a natural sack which lies between structures that need to slide freely over each other, e.g. tendon and bone. It contains a small amount of lubricating fluid. These commonly become inflamed and swollen, leading to a condition known as 'bursitis'.

Shoulder injury

The shoulder is a complex structure with two main functions. Firstly, it must guide the arm and hand through a wide range of movements with precision, such as those needed when passing or catching. Secondly, it must transmit large forces from the upper limb to the body, such as those needed during scrummaging or mauling. The large range of movements that the shoulder can go through, coupled with the forces that it has to withstand, particularly during tackling, make it susceptible to injury.

There are two joints within the shoulder area: the gleno-humeral (or true shoulder) joint between the humerus bone of the upper arm and the scapula or shoulder blade which is constructed like a ball in a shallow socket, held in place by strong muscles and ligaments; and the acromioclavicular joint (AC) joint which connects the shoulder blade to the clavicle (or collar bone) and is often injured following a fall on to the shoulder.

Shoulder instability

Acute dislocation of the gleno-humeral joint often results from an awkward fall or tackle. There is acute pain and deformity and the player will not be able to move his arm. The shoulder should not be relocated on the pitch by an enthusiastic bystander, but the arm should be supported and the player taken immediately to hospital. Fractures or other complications can then be excluded. Reduction will be carried out under sedation or general anaesthetic. The shoulder will be immobilised initially and should then undergo a course of physiotherapy and rehabilitation to strengthen the muscle support before attempting to return to play.

If dislocation becomes recurrent, particularly in younger players, it may be necessary to stabilise the shoulder with surgery. However, in players who have had previous injuries the shoulder may slip in and out ('recurrent subluxation') rather than truly dislocate. There may be a sudden click, popping or dead feeling of the arm which lasts for a few moments and then recovers. This should improve with rehabilitation but occasionally requires surgery.

Depending on the precise details of the problem, there are many types of surgery that can be carried out on the shoulder. In general, either through an arthroscope (key hole surgery) or through an open operation, the damaged shoulder capsule is repaired and often tightened up. Once the structures have healed, physiotherapy is essential to prevent further injury.

Acromioclavicular (AC) joint

This is commonly injured by a fall directly on to the shoulder, often in a tackle. If sprained, the joint remains in line and there is local tenderness and swelling. Partial dislocation ('subluxation') may lead to a small step between the clavicle and acromion, but dislocation will lead to significant deformity. Whilst there are special circumstances which demand surgery, in general the treatment for all grades of AC injury is pain relief and physiotherapy.

Recurrent AC injury, or wear and tear from previous injuries, may give rise to chronic pain in the joint. If it is not possible to control this with physiotherapy or an injection, surgery may be successful with a good chance of a return to rugby.

Fractured clavicle

The ligaments which give support around the joints in children are stronger than the bones. Thus a child is more likely to fracture his clavicle (collar bone) than injure the AC joint. Early pain and swelling settles quite quickly, and 95% of fractures heal over a few weeks without problems. Initial treatment is usually a broad arm sling and pain-killers, leading to mobilisation as discomfort settles. Return to play will depend on the age of the child because the rate at which a fracture heals is related to the maturity of the skeleton.

Right **Figure 6 Shoulder injury**

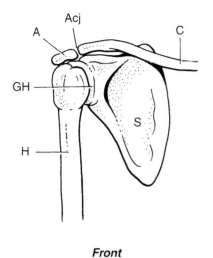

Front

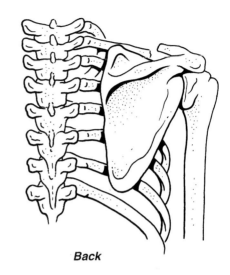

Back

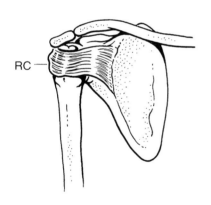

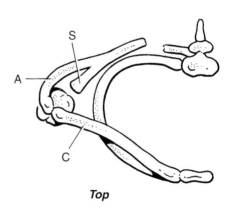

Top

H = Humerus

S = Scapula

C = Clavicle

Acj = Acromioclavicular joint

GH = Gleno-humeral joint

A = Acromion

RC = Rotator cuff

Hand injuries

Injuries to the fingers are common in rugby. They may be pulled and twisted to free the ball in a maul, caught in clothing and wrenched with a failing tackle, or injured when a player falls to the ground.

It may be thought that because fingers are small, injuries are not significant, but a poorly-healed or badly treated finger injury can be very disabling. It may also be thought that because fingers are small, they will heal quickly. The tissues in the finger are the same as elsewhere and take just as long to heal. The structure of fingers and the mechanism controlling both fine movement and strength is complex, and there should be no hesitation in seeking skilled medical care. While accurate assessment, often with X-rays, might indicate that no specific treatment is required, some finger injuries need splintage and a small number may require surgery.

Dislocated finger joints may, because of the obvious displacement, be easy to diagnose and are often easy to reduce. If the joint has been dislocated before, the player may do this himself. However, the joint must be X-rayed afterwards to exclude an associated fracture which is a more serious injury. Finger joint injuries may be very slow to settle down and players may well use tape on the adjacent fingers to give some protection.

Whatever the injury, it is important to remember that finger joints stiffen up very quickly. As soon as healing allows, rehabilitation centred on active exercises under the care of a physiotherapist should begin. Hand injuries vary and while some players are able to return to rugby quickly, it is often difficult to persuade a player to accept prolonged splintage or rehabilitation.

Groin injury

The groin is an anatomical area rather than a single structure, being a crossroads between the trunk and lower limb. Because there are a number of structures which may be damaged, it can be difficult to sort out the origin of the pain and disability. Careful assessment is often needed by a physiotherapist or doctor to target treatment in the right direction.

- The common complaint of 'groin strain' is damage at the origin of the adductor muscles from the pelvis at the inner side of the thigh.
- The hip joint itself may give rise to pain, as can the large psoas tendon crossing in front of it.
- Part of the rectus thigh muscle arises from the pelvis just above the hip joint and is prone to strain with kicking.
- The player may have an incidental hernia (rupture), or sustain small tears of the insertion of abdominal muscles into the pelvic bone.
- The joint between the two halves of the anterior pelvis (symphysis pubis) may become irritated or inflamed (osteitis pubis). This can be associated with excessive symphysis movement.

Most of these conditions will initially respond to physiotherapy and stretching programmes with guided rehabilitation, but on occasions surgery may be needed.

Knee injury

The knee is a large weight-bearing joint which relies on ligaments, tendons and muscle power for its stability. It is regularly subjected to twists or angular strain, for example when the foot is caught on the ground by studs or in a ruck. The most common injuries are to the medial ligament and anterior cruciate ligament (ACL).

On the pitch severe pain or clear deformity will define serious injury. More often there has been a twist and the severity is uncertain. If movement is regained quickly and the player can stand and run without instability, he may continue playing. However, if there is any concern he should leave the pitch and immediately start the RICE regime while waiting for more skilled attention or transport to hospital. It is better not to walk on the knee if it is painful or stiff until it has been checked.

An exact account of the accident is important. For example, there may be a description of the knee cap dislocating and relocating again. The timing of any swelling may also be informative. If this occurs almost immediately it usually implies there has been bleeding into the joint, possibly caused by a ruptured ACL. If the swelling comes up overnight, it will be due to irritation in the joint which usually accompanies a less severe injury such as a small meniscal tear. Tenderness may also indicate the site of injury.

Movement of the knee will be restricted to some extent by fluid, but if it is locked there may be a large meniscal tear. Establishing the precise diagnosis may require further investigation. X-rays can show a fracture but magnetic resonance imaging (MRI) scanning is needed to define ligament and meniscal damage. It may be necessary to examine the stability of the knee under anaesthetic and undertake arthroscopy (key hole surgery) to look around inside the joint. Damage can often be rectified at the same time with arthroscopic surgical techniques.

Medial collateral ligament injury

This occurs when the lower leg is twisted outwards. Different grades of injury may occur. Following a sprain the ligament is not lax and the injury will settle down if the RICE rcgime is followed, along with prompt physiotherapy. A partial tear associated with some fluid in the joint and minor laxity may be treated with a splint before rehabilitation. A complete tear accompanied by extensive swelling and bruising requires detailed assessment by an orthopaedic surgeon with the possibility of further investigation and surgery.

Anterior cruciate ligament injury

Injury to this ligament may result from twisting injuries, often after landing from a jump. The joint will rapidly fill with blood, there will be pain and restriction of movement, and often a feeling of instability. Once it has been medically assessed, the usual approach to management is to follow a graded rehabilitation pro-gramme. The knee will often achieve good functional stability as a result of this.

Should surgery be required, the ACL cannot be repaired directly and has to be reconstructed. The indications for this are persistent symptoms despite intensive physotherapy. The two principle tech-niques of reconstruction are either to use a strip of the player's own patella tendon with a segment of bone attached to the top and the bottom, or to use some of the player's hamstring tendons. These grafts are then threaded through the knee along the line of the pre-vious ACL using either an open operation or arthroscopic surgical techniques.

The tissue of the graft has to regain a new blood supply and assume the function of the previous ACL which, in addition to intensive rehabilitation, may keep the player out of the game for six to 12 months. The decision to go ahead with ACL reconstruction is complex and needs to be discussed carefully with a surgeon who specialises in such techniques.

Meniscal tears

A meniscal tear usually follows a twisting injury. If there is a severe tear such that there is immediate swelling, or the joint is locked, the player should seek immediate attention.

However, quite often the injury seems less serious: early discomfort, and later mild swelling, start to settle down and may even resolve. If swelling or grumbling discomfort persists, or is associated with catching or clunking in the joint, it should be checked. To define meniscal damage requires an MRI scan or an arthroscopy. The majority of tears do not heal and the damaged area has to be removed by arthroscopic surgery. Occasionally a peripheral tear can be repaired.

Right **Figure 7 Knee injury**

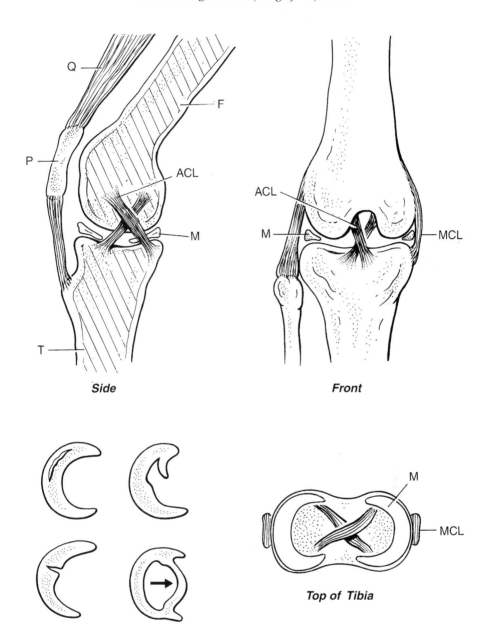

Side

Front

Types of meniscal tear

Top of Tibia

F = Femur

T = Tibia   M = Meniscus

P = Patella   MCL = Medial collateral ligament

Q = Quadriceps   ACL = Anterior cruciate ligament

Hamstring injuries

Poor warm-up and stretching regimes or a marked imbalance between hamstring and quadriceps power will predispose to a hamstring tear. These vary from a strain to a more severe muscle tear. Some players suffer recurrent strains and it is important to undergo sufficient rehabilitation before returning to explosive running. If, after injury, there is no pain on resisted hamstring contraction and no tenderness or bruising, the lumbar spine should be checked, as pain from the lower back can radiate down into the hamstring area.

Shin splints

The term 'shin splints' covers a variety of exercise-related conditions which give rise to pain over the front of the shin. In order to target the treatment properly it is necessary for a specialist to establish the exact diagnosis. In most of these conditions the bio-mechanics of the running pattern and foot function should be checked.

Chronic compartment syndrome is a cramp-like calf muscle pain which increases with running and subsides promptly when the activity ceases. Prolonged rest over several weeks with a slow, gradual return to activity, may allow this condition to subside, though surgery may be required to release the muscle.

Medial tibial syndrome is a pain with localised tenderness along the inner border of the shin bone, which is aggravated by activity and takes a period of days to settle down or may not resolve at all. Rest, ice and injections may help, and occasionally surgery is required.

A stress fracture of the shin bone (tibia) is rare but can occur in response to unaccustomed or unusual repetitive exercise. Pain and tenderness are localised, but scanning techniques are often required to isolate a fatigue crack in the bone. This will settle down with rest.

Sprained ankle

This common injury results from a stumble, when the foot turns over. The severity of the injury varies a good deal but in all cases active treatment and vigorous rehabilitation is needed to restore ankle stability and reduce the risk of recurrent ankle sprains.

Swelling and tenderness usually occur over the outer side of the ankle, anterior to the outer ankle bone (fibula). Initial treatment is with the RICE regime, and if there is concern the ankle should be X-rayed; fractures are usually treated by surgery. In the majority of cases, however, there is no fracture and it is important to see a physiotherapist as soon as possible to begin treatment for the swelling and range of movement. A sprain without a fracture should not be treated by immobilisation. Later on, balance exercises will be used to restore good ankle control and stability before returning to rugby.

Recurrent sprains usually follow inadequate rehabilitation or the failure of the player to keep up an exercise regime. Further rehabilitation is usually effective but the player may need strapping support to help protect the ankle. Surgery is very seldom required.

Achilles tendon injuries

Rupture of the Achilles tendon usually affects players in their thirties and occurs without any warning. There is sudden pain in the back of the heel and players often believe they have been struck. There is a loss of power, and swelling with local tenderness develops rapidly. It may be possible to feel a gap in the tendon. Partial injuries of the Achilles tendon are unusual. Injuries are treated using a plaster cast alone, or by surgery before prolonged rehabilitation.

Inflammation of the Achilles tendon ('Achilles tendonitis') is usually due to repeated strain, resulting in local swelling and tenderness with stiffness after exercise. This condition can be frustrating and very slow to settle. Physiotherapy and treatment such as massage and ultrasound may help; surgery is rare.

Cervical spine injuries

The spine has several functions in its position at the centre of the skeleton. The neck (cervical spine) is designed to move the head, which carries sight and hearing, so that the body underneath may act in a co-ordinated manner to incoming information. The thoracic and lumbar spine are responsible for transmitting forces between the upper and lower limbs. In these functions the spine has to be strong and stable yet flexible. Consider the forces and positions that the spine has to adopt, from static propping to providing a lateral pass while running at speed. These characteristics are trained and refined and at times pushed to the limit in rugby.

The spine is unique in having a hard outer structure of bone and ligament which resists injury and surrounds the delicate and sensitive spinal cord and spinal nerves, which are bathed in spinal fluid. Thus, when considering spinal injury it is important to distinguish between injury to the column or skeleton and injury to the nerve structures within. Bone and soft tissue injury will often heal completely and will usually heal with reasonable function. The nerve structures may not recover, however, and if the injury is serious it may result in paralysis below the level of the injury.

The prevention of neck injury is extremely important because the area is so exposed, not only in the front row but also in open play, particularly during tackles. The player must prepare himself by incorporating a regime of neck strengthening exercises, taught by a physiotherapist, into his strength and fitness programme. Technique, particularly front row play and tackling, must be carefully and repeatedly coached.

Comments concerning acute management of cervical spine injury on the pitch are made in Chapter 4. Serious neck injury will be apparent, but the guiding principle is that any player who has sustained a neck injury should not hesitate to seek a medical check or X-rays. It is well recognised that significant neck ligament disruption may not necessarily be associated with marked symptoms. The majority of neck injuries, however, are merely soft tissue sprains which, having been checked, will respond to analgesics, rest and physiotherapy. Muscle strength must be built up before returning to play.

A specific rugby injury is the 'stinger' or 'burner', caused by the momentary compression or stretching of cervical nerve roots as they exit from the spine. The player will experience acute pain, similar to a feeling of electric shocks, and possibly numbness passing down the arm into the hand which may be associated with a feeling of heaviness or even transient paralysis of the arm. These symptoms usually pass in a few minutes leading to full recovery, but nevertheless the neck should be medically checked. If the symptoms persist there may be more definite damage such as a prolapsed cervical disc.

Similar symptoms may be experienced in both arms at the same time, or in both the arms and legs. Even if there seems to be complete recovery in a few moments this is a potentially serious situation and requires investigation and advice from a spinal specialist. This pattern would imply that there has been a momentary concussion of the spinal cord itself, and after a first episode there is an increased chance of a recurrence possibly leading to permanent neurological deficit. Investigation may reveal that the spinal canal is narrow, thus putting the spinal cord within at risk.

Very occasionally a neck injury may result in permanent damage to the spinal cord and paralysis. This is devastating for the player, his family and for the club. Should such a tragedy occur, the RFU can provide advice on how to handle the situation, and on insurance and fund-raising. Indeed, the RFU has close links with former rugby players who have sustained serious neck injuries. Regular meetings are held, newsletters are published and there is a charity dedicated to this group called 'SPIRE' (Spinal Injuries in Rugby Enterprise).

Head injuries

Head injuries in rugby are common. However, as more than 90% fall into the mildest category the real danger is obscured. Head injuries may appear to bc mild at the outset but may rapidly progress to become life threatening. While these secondary complications are very rare, the fact that they can occur following a head injury should be understood and watched out for by players, their friends, parents and coaches.

Concussion, which may not be associated with a loss of consciousness, is classically defined as a transient impairment of brain function with full recovery. However, even after the player appears to be completely recovered, research has shown changes in brain blood flow and metabolism, which may take a week and often much longer to recover. Subtle impairments in judgement and reaction times, which may be difficult to detect, can persist for some time, along with difficulty in concentration and other vague symptoms.

Following a head injury most attention is focused on injury to the brain, however there may be injuries to the scalp, face, nose, ears or eyes. Conversely, an obviously severe injury to the nose, for example, may direct attention away from a concussion which also needs management. Also any player with a severe head injury, particularly if unconscious, must be handled as though there is an associated neck injury.

The nature of head injury

The brain is a soft structure which cannot readily withstand trauma. It is protected, however, by the skull of hard bone within which it is supported by cerebrospinal fluid. Thus the brain can, to some extent, move around inside the skull to absorb shock and impact. However, if the trauma is too great then the attachments which anchor the brain within the spinal fluid may tear, and the brain may bounce up against the inside of the skull causing bruising, or it may suffer internal damage.

To understand the management of head injury requires an appreciation of how the process of damage to the brain may occur.

Primary brain damage

This is sustained at the moment of impact. Thus it cannot be influenced by what we do (other than avoiding the impact in the first place). There are two types of primary brain damage: contusion or bruising of the brain results from direct impact with the overlying skull following a direct blow; diffuse tearing of the substance of the brain, i.e. disruption to the electric cables (axons) within the brain, commonly results from angular forces which cause the skull to rotate.

Secondary brain damage

As this damage is caused by the development of complications following an injury, there is a possibility that we may be able to prevent or minimise it and influence the outcome through appropriate care. Raised pressure within the skull may result from diffuse swelling of the brain as a response to trauma, particularly diffuse axonal injury. Tearing of blood vessels may lead to the formation of a blood clot inside the skull which can compress the brain. Reduced oxygen supply to the brain may contribute to further damage. This may be caused by raised tissue pressure in the skull, low blood pressure (resulting from bleeding due to some other injury), or obstructed respiration.

Clinical features and early management

Assessment on the field (outlined in Chapter 4) may be difficult. It is important to establish the exact circumstances of the injury and take eye-witness accounts. Following a blow on the head, if the player has not lost consciousness and is otherwise normal, he may continue to play.

However, if there is any doubt the player should come off the field and not return to the match; not just because of concern about his head injury, but also because impaired co-ordination, judgement or reaction will put him at risk of further injuries. Any head injury, even a 'ding', will be followed by a period of incomplete recovery. Automatic behaviour may enable the player to continue playing, but afterwards he will have no memory of the rest of the match. This is a clear case of concussion. Rarely, concussed players may twitch their arms or legs, but this very seldom equates to epilepsy. If there has been a brief concussion without loss of consciousness and a full recovery in a matter of minutes, the player may be sent home with a head injury card but must be accompanied.

Players with an extensive laceration, those with persistent signs of concussion, or any player who has not been reviewed by a medically trained attendant, should go to hospital. A companion should go with him so that if he is discharged from hospital he may still be observed.

When assessing head injury, a vital feature is how the situation changes with time. If the player is improving there is less cause for concern, but if he is deteriorating, i.e. he is becoming more drowsy or more confused, then it is increasingly urgent to seek help and get him to hospital. The accepted method of assessing the progress of head injuries is the Glasgow Coma Score (shown on page 50) which measures response.

The Glasgow Coma Score

Eye opening	• Spontaneous	4
	• To voice	3
	• To pain	2
	• None	1
Best verbal response	• Orientated	5
	• Confused	4
	• Inappropriate words	3
	• Incomprehensible	2
	• None	1
Best motor response	• Obeys commands	6
	• Localises pain	5
	• Withdraws from pain	4
	• Flexes to pain	3
	• Extends to pain	2
	• None	1

Notes

(1) The possible range is from 3 to 15.

(2) The lower the score, the more severe the injury.

(3) A falling score with time is an emergency.

Return to play

The current International Board ruling is based on the need to have a simple and universally accepted instruction across the whole spectrum of world rugby, which is applicable by those without medical training.

Regulation 13.6: 'A player who has suffered definite concussion shall not participate in any match or training session for a period of at least three weeks from the time of injury, and may then only do so after being declared fit by a proper neurological examination'.

There are two aspects to this Law which should be emphasised. Firstly, the player should remain away from the game for a minimum of three weeks, which acknowledges the fact that three weeks may not be nearly long enough following many concussions. Secondly, it emphasises the need for the player to undergo a neurological examination before he returns to playing.

There have been many attempts in medical literature to grade the severity of concussion, with the idea that the medical response to this injury, and in particular the delay before returning to play, may be graded. As yet there is no consensus, but in time the regulations may evolve to take account of this research. Nevertheless, it is clear that however long a player needs to stay out of the game following concussion he must be completely symptom-free before returning to non-contact training, and must then remain completely symptom-free for at least another week prior to returning to contact training or play.

Research shows that unless there has been full recovery from a first head injury, there is an increased risk of sustaining a second. Firstly, subtle impairment of function, which may persist after concussion, increases the risk of further injury. Secondly, although extremely rare, a second blow to the head following a concussion, even a minor one, that has not fully recovered can result in much more serious consequences. The brain has already been damaged by the first blow and is more sensitive to the second. This so-called second impact syndrome is more likely to occur in children where particular care should be taken.

The best protection against head injury in rugby is good coaching and proper technique. There is increasing interest in the wearing of 'protective' head gear. Within the current Laws soft, light, unreinforced fabric scrum caps may be worn to prevent abrasions. However, there is no evidence that thin sponge padding within a scrum cap reduces the incidence of concussion or the effects of it. Indeed, there is some fear that the wearing of head gear may give the player a false sense of security and increase the chances of injury.

Infections

Infectious diseases spread. The ease of transmission from one player to another is variable depending on the infectiousness of the disease and the closeness of contact between players. The common cold could spread throughout a scrummage, yet on the other hand there is no known case in world rugby of the transmission of human immuno-deficiency virus (HIV) about which there has been so much concern.

The prevention of the spread of infectious diseases through the close contact and collision of rugby requires simple precautions. However, in the end it is the responsibility of the player who has the infection to keep himself away from his team-mates. To infect your fellow players is indeed foul play. Should there be any doubt about skin conditions, illness, or the consequences of previous medical problems, medical advice should be sought before returning to contact play. Indeed, for some conditions even strenuous exercises and training may be unwise.

Scrum pox

Scrum pox may be caused by a variety of different infective agents, the transmission of which is facilitated by the close contact of rugby, particularly during scrummaging. It may also spread through the shared use of towels and equipment. A variety of bacteria may be responsible which usually respond to antibiotics. Virus strains, for example the herpes simplex virus (herpes gladiatorum) are very contagious but respond to anti-viral cream or tablets. All skin lesions must be checked by a doctor.

Blood-borne infection

Following infection with HIV it may be many years before some individuals go on to develop symptoms of the severe illness known as AIDS. It is important to appreciate that for transmission to occur there must be very close contact of infective blood with an open wound. There is no evidence that HIV can be transmitted by other body fluids, e.g. sweat, saliva, tears, respiratory droplets or sputum. There is no evidence either that it can be transmitted by sharing eating, washing or toilet facilities.

Hepatitis is a viral infection of the liver, resulting in periods of ill-health and often jaundice. Hepatitis B is transmitted through blood-to-blood contact and is more infective than HIV. As yet there are no known reports of transmission through playing rugby. A player who has jaundice, or who could have been infected with hepatitis B, should refrain from playing and contact training. Thought should also be given to immunising players who are going on tour to areas where hepatitis B is commonly found, for example parts of Africa and the Middle East.

Remember that it is much more likely that a rugby player will become infected with HIV or hepatitis through the close contact of sexual activity or through drug abuse rather than through sport.

Prevention of blood-borne infection

• Medical practitioners involved in rugby must educate players and coaches in the nature of these diseases and in the strategies for minimising transmission both within the sport and their social lives.

• Proper wound care is essential. All abrasions (grazes), cuts and oozing wounds present before a match should be covered with an occlusive dressing. Wounds and grazes which occur during a match should be treated immediately if they are bleeding. All blood-soaked clothing including pads, taping and dressings must be changed, if necessary, during a match.

• Players should avoid unnecessary contact with the blood of other players. If treating a bleeding player the attendant must wear disposable gloves and use disposable wipes or sponges.

• All players with a recent history of infection should seek medical advice before returning to play. Those who have had hepatitis B must have their doctor confirm that they are not carriers. It is the player's responsibility not to put the health of his team-mates or others at risk and he should withdraw from the sport if there is any concern. A player with HIV should seek medical help and counselling.

Open wounds

All grazes should be thoroughly cleaned and treated with an anti-bacterial cream or spray. Some may be left open, but if a dressing is required this should be changed regularly. Cuts should be cleaned and explored by a doctor to make sure that there is no dirt caught deep inside. Contaminated cuts may require more extensive surgical treatment and antibiotics.

Tetanus is a potentially serious infection. Poisonous toxin is produced by the tetanus bacterium (which may lie dormant on sports fields) once it gets into a dirty wound. Apart from the proper cleaning and care of wounds, tetanus is readily preventable by active immunisation. Most children should have received immunisation but it is necessary to have boosting doses every 10 years. If there is any doubt about tetanus immunity, players should seek medical advice.

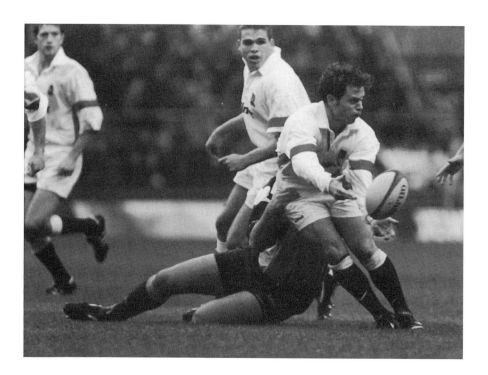

Injury prevention

A major responsibility of medical practitioners in sport is to prevent injury, and the first essential is safe practice both on and off the field. However, injuries are inevitable and it is important to monitor the occurrence of injury and to try to define the precise hazards which lead to them. With this knowledge it may be possible to influence the way that the game is conducted through changes in technique or Laws. Central to this is education of all those involved in the game. The sport should promote insurance cover and support for those unfortunate enough to sustain permanent injury.

Safe practice

Simple, often commonsense, measures are at the centre of prevention. Proper equipment, such as good training shoes and warm tracksuits, allied to a thorough warm-up and stretching regime prior to training or playing, is essential. Particular attention should be paid to those muscles and joints that may already be recovering from injury. Select a soft surface for training, and include a proper warm-down routine at the end to help prevent stiffness.

Players' dress must be safe and should not cause injury either to themselves or other players. The IB Law 4 defines what a player may and may not wear. While protection is certainly afforded by a mouth-guard (*see* pages 58–9) and by shin-guards, there is debate about other items, and Law 4 is currently under review. Padding may absorb impact, but it may also allow the wearer to return too soon after injury or give a false sense of security. The Law currently allows thin pads to be attached to the body by adhesive tape.

Whatever items are worn, there must be no sharp edges or projections such as buckles or clips. For this reason, knee and other braces which are often hinged are not permitted. All clothing or other items which become blood stained must be removed. The size of studs is defined by British Standard, although recent rulings have allowed the use of ridged, rubber-soled boots. It is essential that players read the regulations concerning dress as these are likely to change in the near future.

Monitoring injuries

To know whether safety measures are of benefit, it is necessary to keep a record of injuries. All clubs should keep an injury register and there will be an increasing legal need to do so. On a national level the RFU runs a survey of serious injuries. A form is circulated among all clubs and schools at the beginning of the season, and again mid-season, on which to briefly record the nature of any serious injuries. However, this type of survey does not define the likelihood of a particular player becoming injured. This incidence may only be known if the number of injuries is related to the amount of time the players spend training and playing.

The incidence of injury was addressed in detailed research carried out by a team under Garraway and Macleod in 1995. They studied all 26 senior clubs in the Scottish Borders throughout the 1993–1994 season. 1169 eligible players (96%) provided personal details and recorded all the matches and training they were involved in during the season. Physiotherapists visited the clubs weekly to record details of injuries that had occurred during matches or training. A rugby injury was defined as an incident that took the player off for the rest of the match or training session. A great deal of data was gathered, in particular from the 361 players who sustained injuries. These figures confirmed the impression of previous surveys that half of all injuries are sustained in the tackle (49%). The majority of players (60%) had returned to rugby within a month. The most common injuries were to the knee, followed by the shoulder.

Defining hazards

A potential hazard throughout the game is the mismatch of players. An example was the traditional Old Boys match, when pupils and old boys were mismatched for age, strength and often size and ability. This led to an unacceptable injury rate and the subsequent banning of these matches. Players must also be matched in terms of their training, fitness and particularly position. While many players are able to acquire the skills for several positions on the field, particular training and coaching is required for line-out and scrummage play, especially the front row, and it is potentially dangerous to be drafted in without appropriate coaching.

Influencing the game

An appreciation of injury rates can lead to changes in the Laws for safety reasons. The need to give adequate time for the treatment and occlusion of bleeding wounds led to the rule permitting substitution while bleeding is attended to. High rates of neck injury during scrummaging have led to changes in the rules for engagement, particularly at Under-19 level. Education and appreciation of injuries and safety matters must be imparted to players through education programmes, such as the RFU posters and Player Safety leaflets. Referees, coaches and administrators must be involved in this process.

Insurance

While discussing the prevention of injuries and education, mention must be made of insurance. This is covered in more detail in Chapter 10. It is the player's responsibility to check his level of cover, but he should be encouraged in this by the club, who must ensure that insurance information is available to its members. While the RFU compulsory cover gives adequate insurance for accidental death and disability, some players may feel they need to increase their cover, and additional top-up insurance is available. There is no automatic provision for loss of earnings.

Mouth-guards

It is now universally agreed that mouth-guards are an essential part of rugby equipment. Properly-made mouth-guards provide protection for the teeth, the soft tissues of the face, and the gums, and also help prevent concussions.

Though the habit of wearing a mouth-guard should be encouraged in all players from a very young age, not all mini-rugby players wear mouth-guards and those who do tend to use home-made products. This may be because their coaches played in the days before mouth-guards and are not fully aware of the benefits. Some older players, too, resist or resent wearing this protection. Maybe they want to protect their 'macho' image, perhaps they are less concerned about their already battered appearance, or perhaps they are simply not bothered about injury. All these attitudes are wrong. Teeth are valuable assets and should be protected.

Types of mouth-guard

Over-the-counter

These are usually made of rubber, or one of the plastic materials, and come in three sizes. They are usually loose, ill-fitting and fail to dissipate the impact forces from blows to the head and jaw. They are not recommended.

Mouth-formed (DIY)

There are two types. The first is a hard vinyl shell which is lined with a softer, self-curing material. The shell tends to be sharp. The second is a pre-formed, thermoplastic shell which is softened in very hot water and moulded in the mouth. Burning the mouth is sometimes a problem. Studies have shown that in the majority of cases both these types of mouth-guard are loose-fitting and are only held in place by clenching the lower teeth. They are not recommended.

Custom-made

This is the only type of recommended mouth-guard. Accurate impressions are taken of both the upper and lower teeth, and models are produced from them. The lower model is taken so that the technician making the mouth-guard can register the 'bite' on the under surface of the upper guard. This gives a comfortable fit. It also gives a tight fit so that the guard stays in place should the player suffer a blow to the head.

One of the most common reasons given for not wearing mouth-guards is 'gagging'. The custom-made mouth-guard can be adjusted to prevent this happening.

The thickness of the mouth-guard is important and 2–3 mm is the ideal.

The guard also needs to be of a laminate construction so that the impact forces of blows are dissipated. For those who wish or for those who are sponsored, names or logos can be inserted between the laminates.

Doping and drugs

The taking of certain prohibited drugs, or the use of methods such as blood transfusion, in an attempt to improve performance, is known as 'doping'. Doping is cheating and against the rules and ethics of sport. Nevertheless there are pressures on rugby players to perform better and sometimes to win at any cost. Doping not only ruins the image of the sport but can be dangerous, putting the health of the player and other participants at risk. Drug testing procedures are necessary to protect the sport from the few who may be tempted to cheat.

The International Olympic Committee (IOC) has drawn up prohibitions, guidelines and procedures for doping control, as well as penalties and sanctions in the event of a positive test result. In common with the governing bodies of most international sports the IB has adopted these recommendations. The IB also adheres to the list of banned drugs and methods drawn up by the IOC with the addition of local anaesthetic (*see* page 65).

Within the United Kingdom, The Sports Council, through its Doping Control Unit, is responsible for leading the fight against drug misuse. Education to influence behaviour and attitudes is extremely important and the Doping Control Unit runs information programmes and distributes information packages and leaflets through the RFU. It is the responsibility of the clubs to disseminate information and draw the players' attention to the dangers of drug misuse.

The Doping Control Unit also runs drug testing programmes. While the testing and processing of the specimens is independent, the setting up of disciplinary tribunals and imposing of sanctions is carried out through the RFU. Drug testing may be carried out either within competition or out of competition. For example, in competition two players from each team are drug tested after every international match. At club level players are selected at random and the test is organised with minimal warning. Players can be tested after any match. In out-of-competition testing players can be tested at any time, both during the season and out of season. This testing may take place at training sessions or even at a player's home.

Clubs, schools and players should be familiar with the IB regulations (13.1–5). These regulations are published in the RFU Handbook and it is emphasised in particular that:

13.1.3: " The supply, administration or taking of prohibited drugs by any person is forbidden."

13.1.4: "Any player unable to participate in a match without the administration of drugs or injections to relieve pain or acute illness must be considered unfit to play."

It is very important that players inform their club doctor if they are on long-term medication. Players should also make sure that any medication, whether prescribed by their GP or bought over the counter, does not contain a banned substance.

Banned drugs and doping methods

It is not within the scope of this book to list all the different drugs and methods which are banned, and indeed regulations change with time. Clubs must be sure that they have up-to-date information which is available from the RFU or The Sports Council, 16 Upper Woburn Place, London WC1H 0QP. If there are particular concerns, these can be addressed through the technical department at the RFU. However, doping falls into several categories according to the IOC, and it is important to be aware of these.

Doping classes

(A) Stimulants

Stimulants include drugs which act on the brain to reduce tiredness and to increase alertness and competitiveness. They are banned not only because they stimulate the body mentally and physically, giving an unfair advantage, but because they may produce harmful side effects. They can lead to a rise in blood pressure and body temperature and cause an increased and irregular heartbeat, which could be fatal. In addition, some of these substances such as amphetamines are addictive: examples such as ephedrine may be found, in low doses, in cough and cold medications. Before competition, always check what is contained in medication, even that which can be bought over the counter.

(B) Narcotic analgesics

These are pain-killers. While they may act to reduce discomfort felt from injury or illness, they can be used to deaden pain or mask injury. Thus they may permit a player to play when he should not, and aggravate a pre-existing injury. Misuse of these analgesics may also cause breathing problems, nausea, vomiting and loss of concentration, balance and co-ordination. Moreover they may be addictive. Examples include pethidine and morphine.

Mild analgesics are often found in cold remedies and pain-killers bought over the counter. In the correct dosage they are not harmful.

(C) Anabolic agents

These include various anabolic steroids which are taken to build up muscle bulk with the idea of making the player larger and stronger. However, large muscles are not necessarily stronger or faster. Moreover, these agents can cause considerable harm. They may cause acne, increased aggression, liver and kidney damage, and in males the development of breasts, premature baldness and decreased fertility.

(D) Diuretics

These are drugs which help to remove fluid from the body. They are often used in sports where competitors need to lose weight quickly, but in rugby, where fluid is lost during play, additional fluid loss is unnecessary and could be very dangerous. Some believe that increasing the rate at which urine passes makes it more difficult for the laboratory to detect a banned substance, but this is not the case.

(E) Peptide hormones and analogues

These hormones are substances found in the body, responsible for carrying messages around the body and influencing growth and behaviour. Artificial hormones (analogues) may be used to build up muscles and help healing. Examples such as growth hormone may damage internal organs. Erythropoietin (EPO) may increase the oxygen-carrying capacity of the blood, but there is a danger of blood clotting and strokes.

Doping methods

Techniques such as blood transfusion are more applicable to occasional endurance activities, for example marathon running, rather than the regular sporting involvement of rugby, and are potentially dangerous.

Classes of drugs subject to certain restrictions

Within certain sports and within certain countries, other substances may be prohibited.

In rugby, the use of local anaesthetic by injection to enable a player to continue playing is banned. It is considered dangerous by the IB to inject a painful or damaged area or joint in order that the player be subject to further trauma before proper healing is established. Damage may be cumulative or may become permanent. The only exception to this is that local anaesthetic may be given during a match by a doctor in order to suture a wound (Regulation 13.1.5), in which case drug testing authorities would be informed.

Drug testing procedures

The precise procedures for drug testing are published by The Sports Council and are carefully defined in order to protect the player from any dispute or doubt about the results. A chaperon may accompany the player to the testing room where drinks are available. He is observed while passing urine into a container. The urine is then tested to make sure it is of the right concentration for analysis. The player can select pre-sealed bottles used to transport the urine to the laboratories and divide his sample between the two bottles. Information concerning any drugs which the player may have taken during the previous week is recorded.

Should a sample prove positive, there are procedures for checking the results, defined by The Sports Council, and there are established disciplinary procedures enforced by the RFU.

CHAPTER 6

Training principles and the growing rugby player

The increasing professionalism and globalisation of sport intensifies its impact on the spectator and increases the demand for success. Financial rewards and inducements to players force them to seek greater heights of physical excellence and this is witnessed by the younger athlete who aspires to achieve these goals. These influences are also witnessed by coaches, trainers, managers and parents who seek the accolades and success achieved by our international players. The élite athlete becomes a role model, something to be emulated. The rewards are there to be seen and hopefully touched, but can the growing athlete train in the same way as an adult? Should the adolescent be encouraged to learn and attempt the same training regime as the seniors? In order to answer this question we must accept that the 'growing' athlete is different to the adult or élite athlete by definition. One is still growing, the other is fully grown.

It is well known that selected young athletes can be successfully screened while they are still growing, and given intensive training in preparation for development into élite athletes. However, if this programming is not structured then casualties will occur and permanent damage to the athlete may result. This is not an accepted risk in society and every step should be taken to safeguard the development of our young in sport. If the programming is scientifically and ethically structured with sufficient financial support, then it is an excellent and most effective way of producing an élite athlete.

Training for the young in rugby football is structured primarily by the technical staff of the RFU in conjunction with a national coaching scheme, and relayed to the clubs, schools and teams. Other countries also organise their sport through a central body with government support for academies of excellence. This means that training advice in this country may come from several sources depending on the experience and expertise of those delivering the programming, and consequently it may vary.

The growing athlete

There are certain principles that must be applied when considering the growing athlete. We grow in four stages and this growth, which takes place in the bones, also affects the joint surfaces and the loco-motor system, i.e. muscles, tendons, ligaments, nerves and the blood vessels.

Each individual will have their own characteristic growth pattern, hence the diversity in size and shape at corresponding ages; the sequence does not change, only the time differs. This is the problem regarding sport, sports injuries and the growing child, and hence the approximation of the length of each growth stage. There may well be a four year difference between the chronological (actual) age and the skeletal (bone growth) age of an individual. The development of secondary sexual characteristics may act as an indicator in helping to assess the pubescent stage.

The four stages of growth are:

	Age	
	Male	**Female**
Pre-pubescence	12	10
Early pubescence	14	12
Mid-pubescence	16	14
Late pubescence	18	16
Peak growth (2 year duration)	14	12

It is important to remember that the growing child's joints, joint surfaces and long bones are not the same as an adult's and consequently cannot take the same stresses. This also means that the child's injuries are potentially different to those of an adult.

The shiny, slippery surface lining the joints (hyaline cartilage) is also immature during the growth stages and does not consist of the same properties as mature articular cartilage. One of these properties is the dispersal of impact forces, but in the young athlete these peak forces are transferred directly to the underlying bone, which may damage its development or structure. Excessive high intensity impact forces should therefore be avoided as the bone damage could be permanent and may also predispose to the early onset of arthritic changes. The stability of a joint will also differ during growth and consequently the resultant injury from a similar extrinsic force may injure different structures.

During the pre-pubescent stage, the growth plates are strong and fairly inactive, but through early and mid-pubescence they become very active and are weakened. Finally the growth plates stop growing, fuse, and take on the characteristics of an adult skeleton.

So, if an excessive force is applied across the knee joint during a collision or tackle, the structures may be injured in the following way.

- **Pre-pubescence** - ligaments would be injured as the bones are strong.
- **Mid-pubescence** - growth plates would be injured as they are weaker than the ligaments.
- **Late pubescence** - ligaments would be injured as the bone is now strong as the growth plates fuse.

The skeleton has growth plates but the soft tissues do not; they grow by increasing the number of cells (hyperplasia) or increasing the size of the cells (hypertrophy). As the skeleton grows, and this may be several centimetres during peak growth, the soft tissues have to adapt to accommodate the increase. The ligaments and associated structures are literally put on stretch, creating joint and muscle stiffness.

This is a particular problem for the early and mid-pubescent athletes as this stiffness may cause muscle imbalance, postural abnormalities, biomechanical changes and lead to intrinsic injuries, e.g. anterior knee pain, back pain or tibial compartment syndromes.

An increase in the intensity of flexibility for the whole body using general muscle strengthening exercises, especially multi-joint movements, should be programmed into the schedule of these athletes. Hypertrophy of large muscle groups, especially the antigravity or postural muscles, using resistance exercises, will help prevent adaptations to faulty posture.

Can adolescents train the same way as adults? The answer is no. Can adolescents participate in resistance training? The answer is yes.

Growth and strength

Analysis of resistance training for children has reported that a well-designed, scientifically-based training programme, structured to take into account the skeletal and chronological ages of the children, can have an enhanced effect beyond that which is normally due to growth.

A 30–50% gain in strength can be achieved following an 8–20-week resistance training programme, and children as young as six can be incorporated into this regime. Absolute strength, which is muscular strength unrelated to body weight, will increase with resistance training, but these gains are proportional to the developmental stage of growth, the maximal gain being achieved by adults and the least by the pre-pubescent athlete.

To compare the strength of different people, particularly when considering growing children, the following may be considered.

$$\text{Relative strength (RS)} = \frac{\text{Absolute strength (AS)}}{\text{Body weight (BW)}}$$

Athletes with small body dimensions have a greater relative strength to those with larger dimensions, e.g. the light gymnast may well be able to perform 30 or more pull-ups whereas the rugby prop would find it difficult to achieve that number.

If the large person reduced his body fat (not that I am implying that props are fat!) then his relative strength would increase without changing his absolute strength.

The Rugby Union Fitness Team headed by Don Gatherer, Carl Johnson, Paul Dickenson and Dave Reddin, use this formula for their élite athletes and have designed a training programme that will increase absolute strength without gains in body weight. This principle will have a dramatic effect on increasing the relative strength of a rugby player.

For example, if a player can 'power clean' 160 kg of force and has a body weight of 80 kg then his relative strength is:

$$\text{RS} = \frac{\text{AS}}{\text{BW}} = \frac{160}{80} = 2$$

If that same athlete increases his absolute strength by lifting 240 kg but does not gain weight, then his relative strength increases:

$$\text{RS} = \frac{\text{AS}}{\text{BW}} = \frac{240}{80} = 3$$

If he now reduces his body weight by 5 kg through fat reduction then his relative strength will again increase:

$$RS = \frac{AS}{BW} = \frac{240}{75} = 3.2$$

This is the formula for 'power' à la Jonathan Edwards, and is also why Olympic lifters train above their competition weight and diet just before the event.

Two of these factors influence children as they grow.
(1) Their body mass increases (BW).
(2) Their muscle mass increases (AS).

The first will lower relative strength, the second will increase it. The interaction of these concurrent processes will determine the strength increase or decrease of the adolescent and will play an important role in his development. A structured resistance training programme is therefore desirable.

If you lift maximal weights or work against a maximal resistance it has several effects on the body. There will not only be an increase in muscular strength and size, but an increase in the mechanical or tensile strength of the tendons, ligaments and their bony attachments. Density of the bone is also increased by raising its mineral content. This improvement in muscular strength increases the muscles' ability to absorb energy during activity far more than a weak muscle which would break down. This is an important factor in injury prevention. To achieve this the training must be structured.

Three year rule

The three year rule is popular among experienced coaches. According to this rule, an athlete should use strength-specific exercises and exercises with a barbell, e.g. squats, only after three years of preliminary general preparation. Athletes can learn the technique of all the lifts but should not participate in detailed maximal or sub-maximal lifting programmes.

Overview

To plan and deliver a training programme with a view to reducing the risk of injury, attention should be paid to the following points.

- Muscle groups and joint movements.
- Muscle tendon balance.
- Co-ordination patterns.
- Sport-specific techniques.

Muscle groups and joint movements

Normal functional activities are generally dependent on groups of muscles co-ordinating a movement through a desired range of motion. In order to carry out this movement certain groups or individual muscles may have to act as stabilisers or modifiers to allow the execution of the intended movement. Depending on the sport, some movements will be prime or specific and others secondary or non-specific. It is these non-specific or secondary muscle actions that are often neglected and contribute to injuries. These muscle groups should be exercised regardless of the sport and are primarily the trunk flexors and extensors. Increasing the strength of the abdominals, chest, back and scapular muscles will give a strong fundamental back for successful intensive training. This is particularly applicable to the young during growth spurts to help prevent spinal postural imbalances.

Such basic exercises are:

- abdominals - straight, oblique, and lower abdominal crunch
- back extensors - both arms and legs, opposite arm and leg, prone hyperextensions
- general exercises - press-ups, pull-ups, lunges, standing squats.

These exercises should be performed isotonically as well as isometrically.

To perform any large movements the joints must be sufficiently mobile to allow a full range of movement. Restriction may be due to muscle tightness, joint capsule shortening, muscle imbalance, or an injury, as well as the normal anatomical restraints. With the growing athlete, especially during early and mid-pubescence, the range of joint movements may become restricted. This is because as the skeleton is growing, the muscles, tendons, ligaments and joint capsules are put on stretch and are in effect held in a position of tension. During activities without this full stretch, the soft tissues may tear if excessive force is applied to them.

Excessive repetitive training may also interfere with the development of the joint and consequently produce a muscle imbalance due to restriction of movement.

The priorities during this period of early and mid-pubescence should be to:

• stretch all the joints and muscles
• strengthen and hypertrophy the muscles
• avoid dynamic explosive resistance exercises with weights
• weight train using good technique - full range of controlled movement with repetitions not less than 8–10 per set
• be cautious with excessive repetitive training.

Muscle tendon balance

Growth spurts causing change in the strength, flexibility and rate of fatigue of muscles contribute to the occurrence of injuries in the young athlete. When the muscles are imbalanced, e.g. the quadriceps and the hamstrings, the powerful quadriceps will contribute to failure in the hamstrings, if they are weak, by overloading them. To minimise this risk the hamstring should not be less than 60% of the quadriceps strength.

It is important to recognise that during growth the muscles will become stronger but not in a uniform way. To avoid imbalances an exercise programme should be devised to strengthen all the muscle groups throughout the **whole** range of their movement. These imbalances may not be obvious until the athlete starts to break down during intensive training.

The weakest part of the muscle unit is the junction of the tendon and muscle, known as the musculo tendonous (MT) junction. The tendon does in fact extend into the matrix of the muscle and acts as an anchor for the muscle fibres. At this MT junction the muscle is 'crimped' or folded and it is this delicate formation that allows the muscle to absorb stress. Unfortunately this complex structure is not reproduced after injury and this is probably why 're-tears' occur in athletes with previous injuries to this region. Careful treatment and rehabilitation must be applied in the management of these injuries to avoid a chronic state. Avoidance of injury is critical.

Co-ordination patterns

Inter-muscular co-ordination

All exercises require the co-ordination of numerous muscle groups whether agonists, antagonists, synergists, fixators or stabilisers. These movements may be performed in a controlled way or an automatic way. The learning of multi-joint, multi-faceted movements may be 'chunked' into repetitive controlled patterns. This will stimulate the central nervous learning processes and the movement will eventually become automatic. The greater the number of practices, the better the athlete will perform the movement.

Intra-muscular co-ordination

Skeletal muscle basically consists of two main fibre types - slow twitch (ST) and fast twitch (FT). (There are further subdivisions of FT fibres but they are not considered for this intra muscular co-ordination description.) Each muscle is contracted by a motor unit (MU) relative to its type. These motor units obey the all-or-non 'law'; that is they are either active or inactive.

ST fibres and MUs are specialised for slow, sustained movements with low velocities, while the FT fibres and motor units are the opposite - fast, strong, rapidly fatigued and larger than the STMUs. All human muscle contains FT and ST fibres: the ST are aerobic and the FT anaerobic.

During a voluntary contraction the small STMU's are contracted first, then as the stimuli are increased the FTMUs are brought into play. This is known as 'recruitment' and trained athletes using strength and power training are able to recruit all their FTMUs, whereas an untrained athlete cannot.

Variations of the recruitment order can occur, a technique developed and utilised by Carl Johnson.

The frequency of discharge of the MUs for gradation of muscle force varies according to the force and power produced. In small muscles the most MUs are recruited at levels of force less than 50% of maximum and any increase after this is by rate of firing. In large muscles, MUs are recruited in up to 80% of maximum force with further increases of force again achieved by rate of firing. This is known as 'rate coding'.

Normally the MUs work 'asynchronously' (i.e. not coinciding in time) to produce a smooth action, but élite power athletes can actuate a synchronous action during maximal lifts.

The development and co-ordination of the inter- and intra-muscular patterns are vital in producing maximal power. Examples of people performing superhuman feats of strength are frequently reported in newspapers during life threatening incidents. These feats are achieved by maximal stimuli and minimal neural inhibition.

Development of the neural pathways during growth periods reduces susceptibility to injury, as it makes the muscle, tendon and joint nerve endings more responsive to stimuli. For example, balance training using uneven, narrow or unstable surfaces will stimulate the nerve endings around the ankle joint which will reflexively cause a compensatory contraction of the muscles in the foot and lower leg. Controlled repetitive jumping with different foot placements on an undulating surface will stretch the muscles on each landing and stimulate a stretch reflex. (Sudden stretching of a muscle will cause it to contract quickly and strongly by stimulating and triggering more nerve endings.) This stretch shortening cycle is an important factor for strengthening muscle tissue.

This, combined with good muscle strength and flexibility, will help to prevent ankle injuries

Sport-specific techniques

Rugby has a diversity of technical requirements, some common and others position-specific. Trainers and coaches must have a full understanding of these variations and apply them to their training programming relative to the Laws, equipment and suitability of the player .

Suitability of the player in rugby is of paramount importance for the avoidance of injury. Assessing the age of a young rugby player poses many problems because the chronological age may not match the biological age. For example, a chronological age range of 13 to 15 may include a biological age variation of 13 to 19 years. In other words, some children mature and grow quicker than others and their growth plates may be fusing or growing at the chronological age of 15.

It is good practice in rugby to always remember that the growing player is different from the adult and must be treated accordingly.

Organising groups relative to age, height and weight for games involving physical contact and confrontation will go a long way to avoid injuries. The exception to this is aerobic training, because although the adolescent athlete cannot generate the full aerobic capacity of an adult, it is **not** size related. Resistance training programmes should be designed relative to the requirements of the player and the sport.

Coaches have designed and published a variety of skills and exercises which are all valid for sport-specific rugby training. These combinations are only limited by one's imagination and creativity.

Resistance training - general principles

The relative improvement of strength gains will be less in the pre-pubescent stage than the following stages because the hormonal influences on muscle hypertrophy are not fully operational. Strength gains will originate from stimulation of the neuromuscular system. Development of this neuromuscular system by neural stimuli from co-ordinated 'proprioreceptive' (joint sense) single and multi-joint movements, has a greater role to play than just lifting the weight. This is the period when **technique** should be taught and learnt, e.g. dead lift, bench press, hang clean, cleans and snatches - not with weights but with a light bar or pole. Correctly co-ordinating a multi-joint movement and the consequential elimination of bad or faulty positioning will pave the way to the next stage of development when resistance can be added. This should remain a fun stage, with an emphasis on technique and the laying down of good training practices.

Sustained repetitive movements can still stress the structure of the soft tissue and must be used with care, as the young athlete may develop tendonitis and other related over-use or stress injuries. Training should therefore be broken up into segments or macro cycles composed to cover training technique, games, stretching, strengthening. Such training should always be enjoyable.

Training programming for the adult and growing rugby player should be organised around the following guidelines.

- Etiquette.
- Assessment.
- Warm-up.
- Flexibility.
- Technique.

- Integration.
- Periodisation.
- Management.
- Equipment.
- Warm-down.

Etiquette

There are rules and disciplines that have to be taught and observed during training sessions for the comfort and safety of oneself and those around you. Any athlete who is not prepared to obey these rules puts themselves and others at risk and should be removed from the training area.

Everyone should be familiar with the training schedule, equipment, clothing, safety procedures and training area. They must also keep a training diary and update it with a record of the weights lifted. They should be encouraged to report damaged equipment, illness or injury, or any immediate or latent factor that will affect their full participation in the training session. Communication by the coach and trainer with the athlete is as important as the content of the training schedule. Training should be enjoyable but organised, structured and supportive. Do not force a child to take part in resistance training.

Assessment

A medical examination is recommended for children who have possible physical problems that may prevent them from playing rugby or embarking on a resistance training programme. Consideration should also be given to their mental and emotional suitability for compliance to coaching instruction during exposure to the stress of training and playing. The club physiotherapist may well be willing to conduct a physical examination to determine the presence of postural abnormalities, muscle imbalances, skeletal disorders or injuries.

When designing a training programme it must be recognised by the trainer that resistance training will differ for each individual, relative to their specific and general needs.

All participants must acknowledge and declare their unsuitability for training whether it is from injury or illness, e.g. the flu. Failure to do so will inevitably result in ineffective training and/or further injury.

Training protocol must reflect the requirements of the growing child relative to their development. Provided that a scientific approach is applied with common sense, it will prove to be safe and effective.

If there is any doubt as to whether a player is fit or able to fully participate in training or the game, he should be given an appropriate fitness test that will safely stress the player's weakness without exacerbation.

The fitness test should be scientifically structured and designed relative to the particular weakness. It should then be conducted by an appropriate person who has knowledge and understanding of the physical and psychological principles involved, to avoid further injury. Likewise, it is unwise to accept an affirmative fitness declaration from a player who has not trained or been tested where the responsibility lies within the club. Fitness testing of healthy players for personal or club benefit should be encouraged so that progress can be monitored, recorded and evaluated.

Training programmes should be designed for a player's weakness and **not** just his strengths.

For resistance training, the one repetition maximum (1RM) is the most accurate and reliable measurement. Caution must be used when assessing adolescents who are advised not to perform 1RM exercises. Pre- to late pubescents are advised not to go below five repetition maximums in any resistance exercise.

To measure gains in strength and assess 1RM without performing, the following formula is used.

Repetition	% of max. lift
1	100%
2	95%
3	90%
4	85%
5	80%
6–8	70%
8–15	60%
12–25	58%

To apply this formula to the bench press, for example, ask the player to press as many reps as possible with a weight that he knows will allow more than 1RM.

Count the reps and calculate the 1RM as follows. If 154 kg are bench pressed seven times the 1RM will be:

1RM = 154 x 100/70 = 220 kg.

Maximum power can consequently be assessed with minimum risk.

Conversely, having assessed the 1RM, the exercise may require a specified set, rep and maximum weight percentage.

The chart below can be used for calculating both measurements. The first column is the maximum weight; the other columns the percentages of that weight in kg.

Therefore, if 4 reps max. at 90 kg equals 85% of max.: find 90 in the 85% column and go to the first column to calculate a 1RM of 105 kg.

Weight percentages chart (to the nearest 2.5 kg)

Kg	60%	65%	70%	75%	80%	85%	90%	95%
30	20	20	20	22.5	25	25	27.5	27.5
35	22.5	25	25	27.5	27.5	30	32.5	32.5
40	25	27.5	30	30	32.5	32.5	35	37.5
45	27.5	30	32.5	35	37.5	40	40	42.5
50	30	32.5	35	37.5	40	42.5	45	47.5
55	35	35	37.5	40	45	47.5	50	52.5
60	35	40	42.5	45	47.5	50	55	57.5
65	40	42.5	45	47.5	52.5	55	57.5	62.5
70	42.5	45	50	52.5	55	60	65	67.5
75	45	47.5	52.5	55	60	62.5	67.5	72.5
80	47.5	52.5	55	60	65	67.5	72.5	75
85	50	55	60	62.5	67.5	72.5	75	80
90	55	60	62.5	67.5	72.5	77.5	80	85
95	57.5	62.5	67.5	72.5	75	80	85	90
100	60	65	70	75	80	85	90	95
105	62.5	67.5	72.5	77.5	85	90	𝟿𝟻	100
110	65	70	77.5	82.5	87.5	92.5	100	105
115	70	75	80	85	92.5	97.5	102.5	110
120	72.5	77.5	85	90	95	102.5	110	115
125	75	82.5	87.5	92.5	100	105	112.5	120
130	77.5	85	90	97.5	105	110	117.5	122.5

135	80	87.5	95	102.5	107.5	115	122.5	127.5
140	85	90	97.5	105	112.5	120	125	132.5
145	87.5	95	100	107.5	115	122.5	130	137.5
150	90	97.5	105	112.5	120	127.5	135	142.5
155	92.5	100	107.5	115	125	130	140	147.5
160	95	105	112.5	120	127.5	135	145	152.5
165	100	107.5	115	122.5	132.5	140	147.5	157.5
170	102.5	110	120	127.5	135	145	155	165
175	105	112.5	122.5	130	140	147.5	157.5	167.5
180	107.5	117.5	125	135	145	152.5	162.5	172.5
185	110	120	130	137.5	147.5	157.5	167.5	175
190	115	122.5	132.5	142.5	152.5	162.5	170	180
195	117.5	125	135	145	155	165	175	185
200	120	130	140	150	160	170	180	190
205	122.5	132.5	142.5	152.5	165	175	185	190
210	125	135	147.5	157.5	167.5	177.5	190	200
215	130	140	150	160	172.5	182.5	192.5	205
220	132.5	142.5	155	165	175	187.5	197.5	210
225	135	145	157.5	167.5	180	190	202.5	215
230	137.5	150	160	172.5	185	195	207.5	220
235	140	152.5	165	175	187.5	200	210	222.5
240	145	155	167.5	180	192.5	205	215	227.5
245	147.5	160	172.5	182.5	195	207.5	220	232.5
250	150	162.5	175	187.5	200	212.5	225	237.5
255	152.5	165	177.5	190	205	215	230	242.5
260	155	170	182.5	195	207.5	220	235	247.5

Warm-up

A 15-minute warm-up should be used before beginning training.

The aim of the warm-up is to:

- raise the body temperature and heart rate
- increase the blood flow through to the muscles, joints, tendons and ligaments
- prepare the body physically and mentally for exercise
- assess the body's capability or restriction (i.e. injury) to progress to a higher level of activity.

If the warm-up is not completed then the athlete should proceed no further but be re-assessed and either withdrawn or given an appropriate level of activity relative to his capabilities.

Never miss the warm-up

There is always a risk of injury from an inadequate or ineffective warm-up. A muscle that is not ready to sustain a resistance will either break down or shift the load on to another muscle and cause overload and failure in that group. For example, an injured or tight left hamstring will put stress on the right calf muscle during running in order to maintain an even stride pattern. The result may well be a painful swollen right achilles tendon or rupture of the calf muscle itself.

The warm-up is to prepare the body for exercise only. It is not a flexibility schedule. Flexibility is a technical exercise and the warm-up should be performed before flexibility workouts.

Flexibility

Particular attention should be given to flexibility of the muscles and joints, especially during the mid-pubescent period when the growth rate is at its maximum. The skeleton gets larger and consequently the muscles, tendons and ligaments in effect become taught and require concentrated stretching to avoid adaptive imbalances. If the muscles are hypertrophied in a shortened position, they will remain tight and the athlete will lose his flexibility. This consequently leads to lower back and leg muscle strains, for example.

Stretching is not part of the warm-up but should be considered a separate part of the training programme following the warm-up.

Flexibility exercises during the early and mid-pubescent periods should be accompanied by total body workouts to strengthen the large muscles that will affect joint alignment and posture.

Circuit training fulfills this need and should be incorporated into the training schedule. Also, multi-joint co-ordination movements should be included so that a small increase of weight can be added to the power clean and its components of movement, for example.

The athlete should be encouraged to perform additional flexibility sessions away from the formal training environment.

Auto stretching using body weight, muscle contraction and relaxation techniques, will help to increase the length of the musculotendonous structures. These improvements will be slow; far greater gains can be achieved by using equipment, e.g. pulley systems, or a passive stretch with a training partner.

A training partner can help to give controlled resistance or extra pressure to the stretch exercise using one of the following techniques.

These techniques are based on the physiological principles that:

- the greater the force generated in the muscle the greater the relaxation after contraction.
- contraction of one muscle group (agonist) causes reciprocal relaxation of its opposing muscle group (antagonist).

Hold-relax technique

(i) Warm up.
(ii) Stretch the muscle to the point of tension.
(iii) Partner gently applies pressure to the stretched muscle and instructs the person to isometrically hold that position against the pressure. Do not exceed this force; hold and maintain the position for 30 seconds.
(iv) The athlete is instructed to relax with the partner holding the stretch position.
(v) As the athlete relaxes, the partner should gradually increase the stretch by a small amount to the point at which an increased resistance is felt, and hold that position.

The same process is repeated three to five times using stages iii, iv and v, without releasing the tension.

Force must be removed immediately at the request of the athlete if he feels extreme discomfort or pain.

Contract-relax technique

(i) Warm up.
(ii) Stretch the muscle to the point of tension.
(iii) Partner holds that position and instructs the athlete to contract the opposite muscles to those being stretched to increase the range of movement for 3 seconds.
(iv) Partner holds the increased position and allows the athlete to

concentrate on relaxation in the new position for 30 seconds.
(v) Do not release the tension and repeat stages iii and iv three to
five times.

Again the force must be removed immediately should pain or
extreme discomfort be felt by the athlete.

All increases of movement must be slow and controlled by the athlete as only he will feel the muscle stretch. The partner's force
must never exceed the athlete's force.

After stretching it will be necessary to loosen the muscles with a
warm-down or a further warm-up if other exercises are going to be
performed.

Technique

The coach or trainer must have the ability to analyse the technique
of an exercise, break it down if necessary into its components, and
deliver this in a progressively constructed format that can be performed and understood by the athlete. This particularly applies to
multi-joint movements that require a co-ordinated action affecting
the large muscle groups of the body.

For example, a 'power clean' can be broken up into several components of movement. Each movement is a powerful exercise in its
own right and can be used in the training schedule as an individual
exercise. Acquisition of skill in this way is known as 'chunking'.
Learning progresses by grouping elementary chunks together to
form larger chunks.

Eventually the completed movement can be performed.

1st stage	-	clean pull
2nd stage	-	high pull
3rd stage	-	clean squat balance
4th stage	-	hang clean
5th stage	-	'power clean'

These movements should be demonstrated, applied and corrected
by the coach using a bar or pole without weights, then progressing
to a light weight. If the lifter has difficulties then he should repeat
previous training to overcome his technical problems.

An appropriate load should be chosen for each individual lifter, a load that stimulates the neuromuscular system sufficiently but does not compromise technique or safety. A faulty technique will be carried through to the next stage of training and will become harder to correct. This is often the cause of injures, which is disappointing as it halts the progress of the athlete and is avoidable.

Multi-joint movements are an essential part of programming, but it must be remembered that they should be taught correctly by qualified weight lifting coaches, especially when applied to children, who are still growing and have an immature musculo-skeletal system.

The main purpose of introducing the multi-joint movements of Olympic-style lifts is to develop the neuromuscular system through the advancement of skills, co-ordination and proprioreceptive neuromuscular facilitation (PNF). In other words, to get a 'familiar feel' for the equipment and the movement.

Note: all resistance training must be supervised.

Integration

Training should be integrated to incorporate all the physical and physiological aspects of exercise. This does not mean that you can cover all these aspects in one session; you cannot train for strength and endurance at the same time. The physiological response to this is to produce something in the middle so that the muscle has modified strength with a degree of resistance to fatigue, i.e. type IIA (FT resistant). However, the **endurance** muscles are type I (ST) and the **strong explosive** muscles are type IIB (FT 'fatiguable').

To integrate the endurance and power aspects of training, a mesocycle may be reduced to three weeks and each mesocycle could be alternated:

3 weeks predominantly endurance type I
3 weeks predominantly power type IIB.

Circuit training can also be used to stimulate the type IIA muscle. This will act as the integrated link between the two targeted specialised muscle groups and is useful for team sports lasting 60 minutes or longer.

Note: type IIB power training is for advanced lifters and the 3 year rule applies.

Periodisation

Resistance training should be designed so that volume intensity and loads are varied over a whole year.

This variation in exercises is known as periodisation and comprises:

workouts and training days	=	microcycles
2–6 week training period	=	mesocycle
9–12 month period	=	macrocycle.

One approach is to design a programme that lasts for one mesocycle of 4–6 weeks, and on completion change the contents for the next mesocycle. Continue for a whole year (macrocycle), when the gains and improvements can be analysed, before moving on to the next advanced macrocycle.

Exercise the large muscles before the small muscles.

Do not train if there is fatigue or the presence of delayed onset muscle soreness (DOMS) from the previous training session. Do not do too much in the workout but target different areas during the microcycle.

Muscles will perform better during resistance training when they are fresh, unlike endurance training where greater tolerance to exercise is desirable with a decrease in the rate of fatigue of the muscle.

For example, to incorporate the 'power clean' into a macrocycle by chunking, the components could be introduced with a macrocycle of one year, a mesocycle of 5–6 weeks, and two microcycles per week.

1st	Mesocycle (5–6 weeks)	clean pull
2nd	"	high pull
3rd	"	clean squat balance
4th	"	hang clean
5th	"	clean pull, high pull
6th	"	clean squat balance, hang clean
7th	"	clean pull, high pull, clean squat balance
8th	"	clean pull, high pull, clean squat balance hang clean
9th	"	power clean

Equipment

Various exercise equipment and methods for resistance training of the young athlete have been tried and tested over the years. They have all been effective and are chosen relative to the experience of the coach, accessibility of the equipment, requirement of the sport, and socio-economic status.

Some of this equipment, the machines in particular, are built for adult-size training footwear and do not fit the young or small athlete. If these machines cannot be adapted by pads, etc. then they should be used with caution or avoided altogether, as the lever arm and axis of movement will not correspond to those of the child. This will impose a non-aligned movement and put adverse stress on the muscle and joints, predisposing to injury. Machines are now being produced for the young athlete, and it is advisable that schools/gym clubs should seek out these companies and consider the merits of the adaptations.

Before a training session starts a full inspection of the equipment should be carried out to confirm that it is safe and serviceable. Any faults should be corrected, otherwise that exercise should be eliminated from the routine. Everyone using the equipment must be familiar with it and comfortable with the particular exercise. Always keep the training area tidy and leave the equipment in a safe state ready for the next person.

The disadvantage of machines is that they train muscles but not movement.

Warm-down

After exercise or sport there are two choices. The first and easiest is passive recovery, most people's choice after a heavy workout or demanding game as you simply do nothing and have a shower! This is not the best selection, however, as it does not aid recovery.

During exercise the muscles produce waste products in the form of lactic acid. Lactic acid is the end product of glycolysis, a process which provides energy anaerobically in skeletal muscle during heavy exercise. The anaerobic muscles are the FT muscle fibres, and are also known as glycolytic as they extract their energy from glucose, and glycolysis is the extraction of usable energy from glucose.

Moderate elevations of blood lactate occur during heavy exercise and it is desirable to disperse it. Excess lactic acid will impair the contraction process of skeletal muscle - only a limited amount of lactic acid can accumulate in the muscle before it inhibits contraction.

The second choice is active recovery. Continuing the warm-down by jogging and gently stretching for 15 minutes will help the transfer of lactic acid into the extra-cellular fluid to be dispersed by the blood stream. This will aid recovery considerably by removing lactic acid from the muscle.

The warm-down is especially important for the young athlete who has an undeveloped anaerobic system.

CHAPTER 7

Coaching: good and bad practice

The coach and safety

All measures which increase safety and reduce the risk of danger of injury must be incorporated into the Club coaching programme. These are detailed in the RFU's Player Safety leaflets.

The coach's responsibilities

Player preparation
• Physical conditioning.
• Pre-match or pre-session warm-up.
• Technical preparation.
• Appropriate playing and training kit.

The coach's and the club's responsibilities

Grounds and surrounds
Before any coaching or playing takes place the coach should ensure that:
• potential hazards are removed, e.g. glass, dog mess, litter
• posts are cladded and flags are flexible
• perimeter hoardings are safely spaced
• the playing surface is safe, i.e. not frozen, baked hard by the sun, or waterlogged.

Medical care
The coach must:
• ensure that there is someone who can administer First Aid at the session/match
• know where the First Aid box is and what is in it, and the location of the stretcher in the unlikely event that it should be needed
• if in any doubt, always consult a doctor or the emergency services.

Player preparation

Physical conditioning
With young players, body conditioning exercises are necessary to minimise injury and prepare them for training sessions and mini-rugby games. The aims of these exercises are:

- to prepare tendons and ligaments for the increased muscle bulk that comes with age (puberty) and so retain a high degree of flexibility
- to strengthen the major muscle groups which protect internal organs and vulnerable joints.

Even young children should be encouraged to improve their aerobic fitness (heart/lung efficiency). This can normally be achieved in the training session if the coach plans for maximum purposeful activity. As the children approach and pass through puberty, however, it may be that some specific work will have to be incorporated in the programme in order to give the player a sound aerobic base.

These exercises are detailed in Player Safety leaflet no.8.

Pre-session warm-up
Prior to any exercise the players should take part in a strictly-controlled warm-up. Players must be encouraged to follow well-defined routines.
- The warm-up is better performed on a soft to firm surface rather than on concrete.
- After a gentle jog to increase blood flow to the muscles, specific stretching exercises should be undertaken.
- The range of stretching exercises are outlined in Player Safety leaflet no.8.

Technical preparation
The coach must ensure that:
- the correct techniques are taught and continously practised
- with young players, correct techniques in the tackle and in the body position for the scrum, ruck and maul are rehearsed before each game.

See Player Safety leaflet no.4. N.B.: correct technique enhances safety.

Appropriate playing and training kit
- Players must be encouraged to have their kit regularly washed.
- They must wear boots which conform to the RFU regulations regarding studs.
- Professionally-made mouth-guards should be worn for training and playing.
- Players must never chew gum.
- Jewellery of any kind must not be worn.
- It is recommended that all players, but especially the front five forwards, should wear shin-guards.
- All players should consult their family doctor about tetanus injections.

Figure 8 Appropriate playing and training kit

Mouth-guard fitted by a dentist

Regular tetanus injections

Thoroughly warm up

Wear shin-guards for protection

Simple protective ankle strapping

Legal studs in good condition

The coach in action

The role of the coach is to provide an environment which allows players to learn and develop at a speed commensurate with their potential.

Coaches working with young players must remember that they are not mini-adults: their needs are very different to those of the first team player. Therefore, information needs to be presented in a manner which educates, excites and provides the stimulation required to succeed. The basis for such coaching situations is play. Youngsters want to take part in games so the more fun provided in training and coaching situations, the more likely it is that players will want to return for the next session.

An approach based on playing with complementary skill development is called whole-part-whole teaching, a method encouraged in the RFU Coaching Awards, especially those relating to young players. The youngsters are put into a game situation and are allowed to 'have a go'. The coach identifies any strengths and weaknesses of either the individual or unit. If necessary, they are then given a range of drills such that the coach can observe the weak skill being constantly practised. This helps the coach to isolate the weakness and effect an improvement. The game then continues with the skill hopefully much improved.

It is not good practice to use drills which have no relevance to a player's previous performance. Drills for drills sake are counter-productive in many cases. Coaches who slavishly copy drills out of publications and expect players to improve are often disappointed by the results. Indeed, such practice is often for the benefit of the coach rather than the player.

The psychology of the coaching and playing situation also needs to be examined. It is very unusual for children not to feel some pain during the rough and tumble of a practice session or match. A sympathetic glance, comment or action which reassures a player has tremendous healing qualities. The 'take it like a man' attitude shown by some coaches to players has no place in the teaching of the game, and is responsible for many youngsters not wishing to continue.

As with most complex games, there is tremendous potential for cheating. Coaches who condone or encourage cheating are not welcome in the game. Cheating often leads to illegal, foul or dangerous play. The area of most concern is in the front row of the scrum.

Young players who are given 'tips' by the club's first team prop become capable of destroying an opponent in the scrummage, but will often make it highly unstable and very likely to collapse. Coaches must realise that the scrum in the early years is simply a way of bringing the ball back into play - a restart - and should be treated as such.

The coach and the management team

The management of a group of players is best achieved by appointing a management team. Within this group, the coach will have a special role to play. In partnership with club officials the coach should accept responsibility for much of the off the pitch arrangements - fixtures, transport, First Aid equipment and treatment of players, playing kit and equipment, refreshments, valuables, etc.

Hopefully, with the help of parents and spectators, an atmosphere can be promoted in which young players enjoy the experience of learning and playing.

Everyone involved in the game should work within the traditional spirit of the game, whereby respect for the Laws, the referee, team-mates and opponents is of paramount importance.

Anyone, be they player, coach, official or spectator, who does not wish to accept these traditions has no part to play in this sport.

The coach's role in team management

The special role of the coach in the management team is to deal with the attitude, the instruction, the self-discipline and the behaviour of the player.

There are a number of golden rules which should be enforced regularly and rigorously.

Always:
• accept the referee's decision
• play fair
• treat opponents with respect
• win modestly and lose with dignity
• thank the referee and opponents for the game.

The coach's role on match day

Before the game:
- encourage everyone to be punctual
- demand clean playing kit, including boots
- encourage the quality of play and the players' enjoyment above all else.

Then:
- prepare a thorough warm-up, incorporating ball skills and stretching (*see* Player Safety leaflet no.8)
- practise contact techniques.

During the game:
- encourage all players and praise success and effort. With younger players, use the opportunity to teach and coach 'in-game'
- ensure all players have a reasonable amount of time to play in the game
- encourage spectators to give support to each team, and to applaud success by both
- ensure that all of the referee's decisions are accepted gracefully.

After the game:
- ensure that the team applaud the opponents and referee from the pitch
- attend to any minor injuries
- when appropriate, talk to all of the players about their role in the game.

The coach's concern must be the well-being, the rugby development and the interests of all the players in the team.

Coaching awards and qualifications

Course	Target group	Content	Assessed
Start Coaching Rugby Union	Beginner coaches	• Control • Skills & techniques • Small-sided games	No
Preliminary Coaching Award	Coaches of mini/midi rugby teams	• Control - teaching/ coaching method • Skills and techniques • The game	Yes
• Club Junior Coach Award • Rugby Teacher's Award	Coaches of: 15-a-side at Junior age group level	• Teaching and coaching method • Session planning and preparation • Back play • Forward play • Team play • Fitness for Junior players	Yes
Intermediate Coaching Award	Coaches of: schools first teams, colts teams, adult teams	• Forward play • Back play • Team play • Fitness	Yes
Coaching Award	Experienced coaches normally working at club first team team level	• Understanding the game • Planning for rugby union • Strategy and tactics • Positional skills and training programmes • Effective coaching	Yes

Further information can be obtained from the Divisional Technical Administrator's office or the local Youth Development Officer.

It is in every coach's best interest to attend a course and be assessed. A successful candidate will have undergone a procedure which demonstrates sound educational and safety practice.

CHAPTER 8

Technique

Having accepted that the game should be taught essentially as one of evasion, the reality is that at some stage the players will make contact with either a player of their own team or an opponent on the ground. The primary requirement of the players is to understand that static contact is not really of any use to their team either in defence or attack. All contact must be dynamic, i.e. it must move forwards. This keeps the opponents moving backwards, surrendering their territory.

Dynamic contact does not mean hitting into the contact area as hard as possible; this is how injuries occur. Rather it means making strong contact and driving the legs so that there is constant, steady movement forwards. This allows your team to control how the contact area will develop so that your players can release the ball or defend on their own terms. Coaches need to constantly question the players' understanding of their different roles and what they and other sections of the team are trying to achieve.

The golden rule is: **'Shoulders always above hips.'** This applies in tackles, scrums, rucks and mauls. A player's body position in contact requires constant practice and evaluation by the coach. Any player who is unsafe should undergo intensive corrective teaching so that safe practice can be transferred from training to match play.

Making contact with either ground or player is a skill which requires very sympathetic teaching and coaching. For the few young players who enjoy the rough and tumble of the game in their early years, there are many more who require careful and sensitive handling to ensure they achieve a 'confidence in contact' which will stay with them for the rest of their rugby careers.

What follows is a basic checklist of some of the key factors required to perform various skills, effectively and safely. When contact is involved, safety factors are just as important for the ball carrier as they are for the tackler or supporter.

A thorough warm-up is essential before any player begins contact practice.

Contact with the ground

When making contact with the ground, ensure that players:

- go with the impact - this produces a natural roll
- round the shoulder, land on the back
- take the impact with the ground as in a parachute landing.

When making contact with other players, particularly opponents, it is important to remember that the ball carrier should avoid being isolated and should not try to go too far forwards.

Ball presentation

In order to remain standing, or to make progress, or to move the ball on to the supporting players, the ball carrier should:

- keep eyes open, head up, chin off chest
- take a long stride before contact is made so that: (i) a low body position is produced; (ii) the body weight is just behind the leading foot
- shrug the shoulders
- drive from a low position up into the defender's midriff
- keep driving forwards with the legs
- hold the ball so it is well protected by the leading shoulder
- keep the ball visible (and available) to supporting players.

Figure 9 Ball carrier's ball presentation

The role of the first support player

Key factors
- Eyes open, look at the ball.
- Drive in and under the ball.
- Use the opposite shoulder to the ball carrier.
- Share the ball with the ball carrier, i.e. four hands on the ball.
- Drive together.
- Release the ball early so that the support may pass, or run, or roll out and run, or feed.

Figure 10 First support player

The role of other support players

Key factors
- Bind over the first ball carrier.
- Keep a balanced shape - 'far side, near side'.
- Enter maul level with or from behind the rear feet.

One player looks after the ball; the rest look after the ball carrier.

Figure 11 Other support players

Scrummage

Good technique in the scrum is vital if players are to play safely. The basic body position is characterised by:

• head up, chin off chest, eyes open
• back flat, shoulders above hips
• feet back, legs slightly bent
• as many studs in contact with the ground as possible.

This basic scrummaging position is suitable for locking out and also for driving forwards.

To lock out, players would lock at all of the major joints in the leg, and sink at the knees. At the same time, the feet become rather more splayed with the heels turning slightly inwards to make contact with the ground. The grip is tightened and every player squeezes those players they are bound on to.

To shove forwards, the body positions are very similar except the bend at the knee might be slightly more pronounced to allow players to push forwards a greater distance before they may need to move their feet. Players in the second row may play: either both feet back; or one foot up, one foot back. Neither has an advantage over the other - it is largely a matter of what the player prefers.

Figure 12 Basic scrummaging position

Once players understand this basic position and can display it consistently, then the coach can further fine tune it. When looking at the front row players head-on, the coach should see:

- a wide stance
- each individual's shoulders level.

The position which should receive a good deal of technical attention and safe practice advice is that of hooker. Here is a player who is hanging between two other players and is expected to balance on one leg and drag the ball back with the other foot, while resisting the force exerted by the opposition. At the same time, the hooker will be slightly twisted from the waist and laying out of balance across the width of the loose head prop's feet.

Figure 13 Position of the hooker

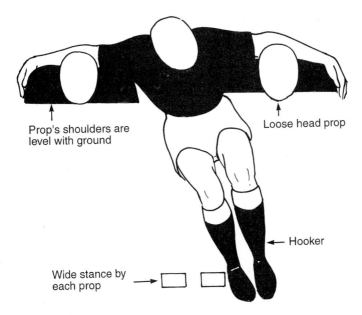

Prop's shoulders are level with ground

Loose head prop

← Hooker

Wide stance by each prop →

It is essential that the player receives technically sound advice and treats the scrum as a restart, not a personal feud with his opposite number. Twisting and lowering an opponent, either at prop or hooker, is inherently dangerous to a scrum and must not be condoned nor encouraged.

Binding, however, is governed by a Law and is an integral part of safe practice. While individuals may have a preference for binding at different heights from hip to armpit, the Laws dictate how players must bind. Technically, players must reach as far as possible around those who they are binding on to, so that the upper arm and forearm are completely flat against the body. This ensures a safe, solid scrummage. Tight binding in the front row is essential to the provision of a strong, stable platform.

Figure 14 Correct binding: each player reaching as far around the next player as possible

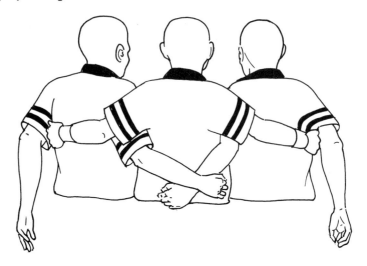

Line-out

The line-out is just another restart and should be treated as such. The Laws dictate that junior players and younger are not allowed to support a player in jumping for the ball. The support players must wait until the player catches it and return to ground.

However, there is still a couple of safety factors which must be considered.

- Players must not interfere with opponents who are trying to win the ball.
- It is better for support players to play with their heads up, looking for the ball, rather than to crouch down with their hands on their knees.

Tackling

It is essential that players take part in a thorough warm-up routine prior to any contact practice.

Young players may pair up by size, although it is recognised that some experienced players will be able to cope with pairing by ability. Consult Player Safety leaflet no.4. Coaches should make steady progress with care and discretion.

When teaching/coaching young players, the progressions which follow are strongly recommended. Teach all basic techniques using tackle bags if they are available. Take into account the fact that tackling a player running at speed requires a bravery that only a few youngsters are born with. All young players can be given confidence in their tackling ability with sympathetic and constructive coaching.

Young players should never be exposed to contact until they achieve not only the competence but also the ability and confidence to control the tackle situation. Safety factors are just as important for the ball carrier as they are for the tackler. Look at the key factors for making contact with the ground on page 98.

Certain key factors must be emphasised when teaching/coaching players to tackle.

Side tackle

Key factors
- Keep eyes open and look at the target.
- Head must be behind the legs.
- Brace the shoulders before contact.
- Keep the head up, chin off the chest and neck firm.
- Make contact with the shoulder on the thigh.
- Drive with the legs, wrap the arms around the ball carrier's legs, grip with the arms and hands.

Figure 15 The side tackle

Rear tackle

Key factors
- Keep eyes open and look at the target.
- Head must be to one side of the legs.
- Brace the shoulders before contact.
- Keep the head up, chin off the chest and neck firm.
- Drive with the legs to hit the ball carrier's buttocks with the shoulder.
- Wrap the arms around the ball carrier's legs and grip with the arms and hands.
- Aim to land on top of the tackled player.

Figure 16 The rear tackle

Front tackle

Key factors
- Keep eyes open and look at the target.
- Drop into a crouch to receive the ball carrier on one shoulder.
- Keep the head to one side of the ball carrier's body.
- Keep the head up, chin off the chest and neck firm.
- From the crouch position, sit and fall backwards as contact is made with the ball carrier's legs.
- Wrap the arms around the ball carrier's legs and grip tightly with the arms and hands.
- Let the momentum take the ball carrier over the shoulder.
- Twist to land on top of the tackled player's legs (to the right if using the right shoulder, to the left if using the left shoulder).

Figure 17 Front tackle

Tackling progressions

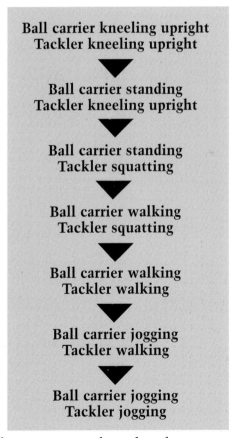

Ball carrier kneeling upright
Tackler kneeling upright

▼

Ball carrier standing
Tackler kneeling upright

▼

Ball carrier standing
Tackler squatting

▼

Ball carrier walking
Tackler squatting

▼

Ball carrier walking
Tackler walking

▼

Ball carrier jogging
Tackler walking

▼

Ball carrier jogging
Tackler jogging

Only progress the sequence when the players are competent and confident in their ability to tackle.

CHAPTER 9

The rugby Continuum

It is said that there is only one game of rugby football and that is the 15-a-side game. This may be true, but to the young and uninitiated the Laws and techniques of rugby union are complex and rather daunting. As a consequence the RFU has encouraged the introduction of mini rugby and the use of the Continuum as a method of introducing the skills of the game. The Continuum should be viewed as a coaching pathway through which each youngster acquires, by gradual degree, those skills required to participate in the full 15-a-side game by the age of 13.

In addition to the progressive nature of skill introduction, the Continuum is also strongly accented towards the safe playing of the game.

The main activity and skills introduced at the earliest age are running with the ball, evasion, running in support of the ball carrier, passing, and running to touch the ball carrier. The emphasis is on running, and games that are played are between teams of small number with a coach participating in a coaching capacity on the field of play. The age groups are normally kept separate and distinct, but if it is a necessity, specific age groups may combine but will be governed by the rules and practices associated with the younger age group.

The RFU coaching manual *Even Better Rugby* is recommended to be used to introduce the skills of tackling, scrummaging, line-out and kicking in a safe and controlled manner. In addition clubs and schools are encouraged to use the Start Coaching Rugby Pack and run courses for the RFU Preliminary Coaching Award, thus encouraging mini rugby helpers to acquire a greater understanding of how they should introduce the game to the beginner.

As the young players mature, the skills of scrummaging are introduced but at the initial stage practice is with an uncontested scrum, with the players learning where to place their head, hands and feet, and the correct body angle. They are not allowed to push.

In the next year tackling is introduced in accordance with the progressive stages described in *Even Better Rugby*. The players begin learning and practising the required skills by paying strict attention to the correct placing of the head of the tackler, the use of the arms and the position of the body. In the initial stages much of the practice is without boots, at a walking pace and if necessary on all fours. The Continuum stipulates at this age group and all others that the hand-off is prohibited. At this age and below, the smaller size 3 ball is recommended to facilitate greater control over handling.

In further yearly stages, tackling and scrummaging is permitted in games with the number of players in a team being progressively increased so that at Under-11, 12 players (five forwards maximum and seven backs) form the team. Until this stage scrummaging techniques have been applied without strength being used, and as the numbers in the scrum are increased coaches are encouraged to pay particular attention to the body position of the front row players and the method of binding and engaging of the second row. The various safety aspects are covered in the Continuum *Notes for Guidance* and in *Even Better Rugby*. In addition, at this age lineouts are introduced with restricted numbers, the Under-19 Laws being applied except that lifting is prohibited on safety grounds.

In addition to the progressive introduction of the various rugby skills, the Continuum provides definite instruction at every age group to enable the player to be coached and participate in safety.

The safety aspects that are emphasised in the *Notes for Guidance* and *Even Better Rugby* reflect the increasing technical ability of the players, their understanding of the game and their physical development. The notes on safety also include the prohibition of lifting in the line-out, the hand-off and all dangerous play. Examples of dangerous play such as swinging by the shirt, using the ball as a battering ram, the two-handed push into touch and others, are highlighted and penalties recommended.

The over-playing of players is addressed by a restriction on the number of games each age group can play plus the duration of the game. Although it is recognised that competition is healthy, the psychological advantage of participating in a healthy, safe outdoor activity without having to win at all costs cannot be over-stated in the development of the young. Although this cannot be embodied in the rules of the Continuum, a restriction on winning margins is included in the *Notes for Guidance*.

Without the supporting manuals on coaching and refereeing, the Continuum's *Notes for Guidance* cannot be utilised to its greatest effect. All three of them are useless without the use of common sense by those responsible for our young players.

Development

As already stated, in order to equip coaches to lead youngsters through the progression of mini/midi rugby, it is essential that constituent bodies, clubs and schools use the Start Coaching Rugby Pack and run courses for the RFU Preliminary Coaching Award, thus encouraging mini rugby helpers to acquire a greater understanding of how they should introduce the game to beginners. This will ensure that the game is enjoyed by all concerned.

The season

The season lasts from September 1st to April 30th inclusive. The playing of mini/midi rugby matches in England by, or between, clubs outside the season (as defined above) is forbidden, except in special circumstances approved by the Rugby Football Union.

Age groupings

The age grouping of players is taken at midnight on August 31st/September 1st at the beginning of the season in which matches are to be played.

Safety

If a player appears injured, the referee must stop play immediately.

- Don't wait for the ball to go dead.
- Don't wait for anything.
- Blow your whistle at once.
- Better to be safe than sorry.
- Obviously, you must use your judgement - players don't want to stop for every slight knock - but you can usually tell when a child appears hurt.
- Take no chances.
- Act fast.

But act with caution. **Do not move an injured player**. In particular, stop other people from rushing in and hauling the player to his feet: they may exacerbate the situation.

Concentrate on the vital things.

- Difficulty in breathing? Make sure the player hasn't swallowed his tongue. If he has, hook it out at once.
- Seems stunned? May be concussed - if so, must go off and have a medical examination.
- Bleeding? Must go off for treatment.

But still do not move the player. Invite him to get up. If it hurts to move, let him stay where he is and **send for expert help.**

Dangerous play can cause injury.

- High tackling (above the shoulders) is dangerous - penalise it!
- Collapsing a ruck or maul is dangerous - penalise it!
- Sloppy scrummaging leads to collapsed scrums - keep the heads no lower than hips.
- Hand-offs and fend-offs are dangerous - penalise!
- Tripping with the foot is dangerous - penalise!
- Hanging on to the ball while lying on the ground is dangerous (to the holder) - penalise!

There will always be knocks and bumps in mini rugby, but if dangerous play is eliminated, then many serious injuries will never happen.

After a stoppage for injury, restart play with a free pass or a scrum to the team that last had the ball.

CHAPTER 10

RFU Personal Accident Insurance Scheme

Background

Some 25 years ago the RFU, conscious of the physical nature of the game, introduced a personal accident policy for players. This was an innovative step since at that time the RFU was the first sports organisation to arrange such cover.

Initially, participation in the scheme was voluntary but in a short time this was made compulsory. This meant that every player representing an RFU member club had to be insured.

Cover

The policy which forms the basis of the scheme is a PTD – Permanent Total Disablement – policy. This means that a qualifying injury must be permanent and total and any condition must be supported by medical opinion. This said, it is a no fault policy and the circumstances as to how the injury was obtained would not be an issue.

Year on year the RFU is committed to improving the benefits payable under the scheme. From fairly modest beginnings the scope and cover provided have been enhanced (*see* schedule on page 112). The only constraints on even greater improvements lie with the premiums that would necessarily have to be passed on to clubs. Grateful acknowledgement must be given to the Trustees of the Wavell Wakefield Youth Trust who subsidise the premium of youth teams by paying 67% of junior insurance, and 86% of mini insurance.

In addition to the personal accident policy, which is basically a safety net for those playing rugby, there are other insurances available either through the RFU or one's own broker. These can be for loss of earnings, private medical, enhanced personal accident, death by natural causes, tour insurance etc. Every person is encouraged to arrange cover appropriate to their individual needs.

Scope of insurance cover for 1997/98 season

	(A)	(B)	(C)	(D)
(1) Death following accidental injury *See* Note 1	£20,000	£11,000	£5,000	£5,000
(2) Loss (including loss of use) of: • one limb • one eye • hearing in one ear	£25,000	£25,000	£25,000	£12,500
(3) Loss (including loss of use) of: • two limbs • two eyes • hearing in two eyes	£50,000	£50,000	£50,000	£25,000
(4) The insured person is unable to carry out current occupation, trade or profession because of the injury – but is able to carry out an alternative (i.e. permanent total disablement from usual occupation)	£50,000	£50,000	No cover	No cover

N.B. Benefit is not available to professional players.

	(A)	(B)	(C)	(D)
(5) The insured person is unable to carry out any occupation, trade or profession because of the injury (permanent total disablement from any occupation) *See* Notes 2 and 3	£250,000	£250,000	£250,000	£250,000

(**A**) 18 years and over; (**B**) Over 16 years and under 18 years
(**C**) Over 12 years and under 16 years; (**D**) Under 12 years

Note 1 Death from heart failure or collapse not arising from accidental injury does not come within the cover. A voluntary option for death by natural causes cover is available.
Note 2 Benefit (4) does not apply if the claimant has not been in regular employment in the previous 24 months prior to the injury.
Note 3 The playing of rugby is not classified as an occupation, trade or profession for the purpose of Section (4).

The Accidental Death and Disability Scheme is arranged on behalf of the RFU by Bowring Marsh & McLennan Ltd and underwritten by Sun Alliance and London Insurance plc.

All application forms for the Accidental Death and Disability Scheme should be returned to Twickenham. All other communications concerning the insurance schemes should be sent to:

Rugby Football Unit (MP10)
Bowring Marsh & McLennan Ltd
The Bowring Building
Tower Place
London EC3P 3BE

tel: 0171 357 3180
fax: 0171 929 2705.

For more information, consult the RFU Handbook.

CHAPTER 11

Women's rugby

Women's rugby was first played regularly in the late 1970s. Today there are over 270 clubs in England, and some run two or even three squads on a regular basis. All these clubs are part of a men's club and many are based at Senior men's clubs.

The game in England is administered by the Rugby Football Union for Women (RFUW) which, apart from the full time National Development Officer, is run by volunteers, many of whom are still playing rugby.

The first England international was played in 1987, when England beat Wales 22-4. The fixture has been played annually since and England have yet to lose to Wales. In 1994 England won the World Cup, beating the USA 38-23. Today, in addition to the England team the RFUW fields England A, England Emerging and England Students: this provides a development route for budding international players.

The RFUW currently organises, in addition to the International fixtures, a National Cup Competition and a six-Divisional League for all Senior clubs. Similar competitions are organised for the Student clubs.

While the RFUW is an associate of the Rugby Football Union, it is self-financing and also provides a personal accident cover scheme. No team is permitted to play women's rugby if they are not adequately insured.

By any standard, the rate of growth of the women's game has been remarkable. As the influx of recruits has increased there has been a significant rise in the number of schoolgirls who wish to play rugby: these girls are therefore feeding into the women's clubs.

Many of these youngsters have played club mini rugby, up until the age of 12 when they outgrew the mixed teams they had been competing in with boys. While the RFUW sees the enthusiastic young players as the future of the game, and is determined that they will not be lost to the sport, it also recognises that there is a need to provide a 'safe' sporting environment for these young players so that they can flourish and progressively build on rugby experience and skills.

In September 1996 the RFUW produced a policy document entitled *Partnership for Progress*, which was devised not only to declare the Laws for full contact 15-a-side junior rugby for girls, but also to embrace the virtues of the RFUW's long term development strategy, which aims to create the most enjoyable and the safest environment for young players.

The RFUW recognise that some teams may have less than 15 players: *Partnership for Progress* explains how to downsize scrums and also details a series of extra safety features for the junior game, such as uncontested scrums.

In order to offer maximum flexibility, officials of the playing teams must have close liaison before each game and discuss and agree team numbers, ages, playing experience, physical maturity and the various non-contact and contact options available.

In addition to this policy document, the RFUW reviewed and continues to review the rules and regulations relating to its competitions, in order that it carries on providing a safe environment in which women of all ages can play rugby.

In September 1996 the RFUW stipulated that no girl under the age of 16 years may take part in the game, training or otherwise, involving any player aged 16 years or over, where full contact is involved. This decision was taken with purely safety in mind and in time, with the continued increase in the number of girls and women playing the game, it is likely that further age restrictions will be introduced.